# Young Adult Literature

# Young Adult Literature

## The Heart of the Middle School Curriculum

Lois Thomas Stover

Boynton/Cook Publishers
HEINEMANN
Portsmouth, NH

**Boynton/Cook Publishers, Inc.**
A subsidiary of Reed Elsevier Inc.
361 Hanover Street
Portsmouth, NH 03801–3912

*Offices and agents throughout the world*

**Library of Congress Cataloging-in-Publication Data**
Stover, Lois Thomas
    Young adult literature : the heart of the middle school curriculum
 / Lois Stover.
       p.    cm.
    Includes bibliographical references.
    ISBN 0-86709-376-5
    1. Middle schools—United States—Curricula.  2. Literature—Study
and teaching (Middle school)—United States.  3. Young adult
literature.  I. Title.
    LB1628.5.S86  1996
    373.19—dc20                       96–9687
                                             CIP

Editor: Peter R. Stillman
Consulting editor: Virginia Monseau
Production and cover design: Vicki Kasabian
Manufacturing: Louise Richardson

Printed in the United States of America on acid-free paper
99  98  97  96    DA    1  2  3  4  5

*For Amanda and Joe*

# Contents

# Contents

# Acknowledgments

I would like to express my gratitude to the following individuals who contributed in their own unique and wonderful ways to the development of this book: Virginia Monseau, for her support and editing and her invitation to write the book; Hal Foster, for his encouraging feedback; Anne Sauvé, for her careful editing; my colleagues in the Secondary Education Department, particularly Gloria Neubert, who had to live with me while I worked on this project; Bob Wall and Lori Reed, who helped analyze data; the middle school teachers who participated in the survey on which parts of the book are based, and especially Rita Karr, Rebecca Joseph, Jackie Sachs, and Stephanie Zenker, who shared their expertise with me. And, of course, my family.

# Introduction

## A Context for This Text

This text is designed to help preserve and inservice teachers develop concept-based, transdisciplinary curricular units that reflect two things: what we know about the need for middle level students to work together to construct knowledge and what we know about the value of putting young adult literature at the center of such a planning process. It is designed to help readers consider the reasons for these recent changes in educational practice, determine the implications of such changes for their own teaching, and increase their knowledge of middle school students. The text also presents an overview of teaching strategies best suited to the synthesis of this evolving knowledge base. As the title suggests, the emphasis is on young adult literature's central place in curricular planning for those students who are, as Nancie Atwell called them, "in the middle" in so many ways.

## Chapter Content

Chapter 1 provides a theoretical and research-based rationale for using transdisciplinary, concept-based units centered on young adult literature in the middle school. It also defines young adult literature, and describes a general planning process for developing such units based on literary texts written specifically for and about young adults.

Chapters 2 through 4 present specific examples of such units, including goals, annotations of the text sets, explanations of the transdisciplinary connections, sample transdisciplinary activities, and model evaluation procedures.

Chapter 5 describes some of the pedagogical strategies most compatible with concept-based, transdisciplinary planning and teaching, and discusses assessment practices that are philosophically in agreement, especially in the ways they reflect a whole language perspective on teaching and learning.

# A Personal Reflection

Working on this text has reminded me of the difficulties inherent in communicating through writing. It would be easier to present the relationships that undergird this book graphically through a triple Venn diagram—three overlapping circles, one containing information about middle schools, one focused on curriculum planning and implementation, and one outlining what we know about the nature of adolescents and their development. At the heart of these circles, in the space defined by their union, is young adult literature: the logical starting point for planning middle school learning experiences. But writing is a linear process; it is difficult to explain a three-dimensional series of relationships on a two-dimensional plane. Thus, at times, I have had to be more prescriptive than I would like. Nevertheless, I hope that middle school teachers and future teachers of the middle grades will be able to take what is in these pages and, working with the students in their classrooms, develop their own exciting transdisciplinary inquiries.

# One

# Young Adult Literature, Transdisciplinary Planning, and the Middle School

After signing a contract to teach English to eighth graders, I suddenly realized how little I knew about middle school students. My student teaching experience and my first teaching position were at the high school level, with students in eleventh and twelfth grades, and I was fairly certain that thirteen-year-olds would have different needs, interests, and abilities than the students I had previously encountered. In trying to educate myself about middle school students, I discovered a rich body of research about them as individuals in transition. I also learned, through that research and later on the job, about the middle school as a unique place in which students at the crossroads between childhood and adulthood could be challenged through transdisciplinary curricular units to seek real solutions to real problems that transcend traditional content-area boundaries. Involving students in such units, I learned, provides opportunities to explore generalizations and ideas in a hands-on fashion without feeling limited by rather arbitrary divisions among the traditional teaching disciplines. Finally, by listening to my students and working under the guidance of a wise English supervisor, I came to appreciate the importance of using literary texts written specifically for the young adolescent, and I began to put such texts at the heart of my efforts to develop, with colleagues, transdisciplinary units. This first chapter describes early adolescence and the connections to concept-based transdisciplinary units *centered on literature written specifically for and about adolescents.*

Recently, I asked my students at the university level—all future teachers of varied secondary school subjects, who also represent several different generations—to complete a freewriting activity based on

1

their memories of their interests, relationships, and attitudes toward school as thirteen-year-olds. They unanimously declared that they were glad they would never have to be thirteen again. While some confessed to having fairly happy, tranquil relationships with their families, all of them noted that their friends were much more important to them during adolescence. It was their friends to whom they turned as they sought to figure out how to increase their independence from parents or guardians, what they believed, what they liked and disliked, who they wanted to be. My students then created group webs on "adolescence" and summed up the results with the following words and phrases: chaotic, a time of becoming, confusion, an emotional roller coaster, in-between, and egocentric.

These same students were assigned to read books written specifically for an audience of middle school students and find passages that seemed to them to epitomize the nature of adolescence. Here are several passages they identified.

When Jason, in *Space Station Seventh Grade* (Spinelli 1985), is taking a shower after P.E.—it is the beginning of seventh grade—all the boys at first dash in and dash out, keeping their fronts to the wall and their backs to the center. But then, one by one, they start turning around. Here's what Jason has to say about what he observed:

> Hair. That was the first thing I noticed. Joe Sorbito had pubic hair. Lots of it. All black, like his head. . . .
>
> What's funny is that Joe Sorbito is little. He's one of the littlest guys in seventh grade. And he's not older than anyone else either. He just has hair. It's a weird feeling being in the shower with him, especially if it happens to be just the two of you. It's like I thought he was like me but I found out he's not. It makes you feel like a little kid again.
>
> I watched him drying off. It's under his arms, too. I wonder what it's like. What does he know that I don't know? (25–26)

What Jason is describing is a universal concern of puberty.

My students also loved Molly, from Rachel Vail's *Ever After* (1994), describing the dizzying effects of trying to "think." Molly, said one future math teacher, is the quintessential fourteen-year-old. Molly says,

> If I can't have any real excitement in my life, I guess anxiety will have to do. I worry that everybody's looking at me. I worry that nobody is looking at me. I worry that I am boring, fat, ugly, not a good enough friend, destined to be an anonymous loser all my life. I worry that it will be hot and I'll sweat uncontrollably and smell or have underarm stains, or that it will rain and my hair will frizz . . . that the democratic process is all just one huge popularity contest,

which means not only that I have about zero chance of ever getting to be president, but also that the people in charge of our national security are grown-up versions of popular kids—a terrifying thought when you consider the brainpower and depth of your average popular kid. I worry that at any moment I might make a total fool of myself in front of everybody. I also worry that maybe all these worries are totally realistic. (64–65)

Molly continues, saying,

It's *now* for so short a time, a totally uncatchable time, because as soon as the thought has crossed my mind, "This is *now*," it's too late; I have already thought that thought in the past. It makes me dizzy. One thing leads backward to the next, and it's hard to figure out where everything started . . .

Molly then goes on to describe the series of coincidences that led to her looking like a jerk, in her mind, in front of Jason, the object of her fourteen-year-old affection.

Maybe that's ridiculous, but it's what I was thinking, and the whole chain-of-events logic made me feel paralyzed, like any move I made could be so impact-ful it would change the whole course of my life. So I sat there on the toilet for I don't know how long, until I convinced myself that that was a decision, too, with the probable next event being that Vicky would think I had diarrhea or something. (91–92)

The summer she is fourteen, Molly wishes in her journal for a friend in whom she can confide every thought and emotion. But best friend Vicky is so touchy; Molly spends much of her time defending Vicky's moods and trying to cajole her out of them. So, when a new girl enters the picture, her presence complicates Molly's relationship with Vicky and complicates her budding sense of self. To date, Molly has been "the nice one." Now, she's tried shoplifting; she's having fantasies about her sax teacher, Vicky's older brother; and she's jealous of a former boyfriend's interest in her new friend. She wants to come to closure on her pre–high school years, but she learns there are no neat and tidy answers. And she shows that she is just beginning to come to terms with that reality when she states, "At least I'm not so vanilla anymore. Stuff happened to me. It's mine" (166).

My class went on to consider some of the teaching implications of their personal reflections and of these literary passages that struck them as typical of their future students' perceptions and concerns. We arrived at the following statement:

Some young adolescents become "good students" as they attempt to create identities for themselves. Some of them do enjoy learning for its own sake. However, most middle level students do not place any great value on school, except as a place in which to conduct their increasingly important social lives away from their families.

These future teachers also commented on the inefficiency of the traditional curricular structure for students of this age. As they tried to relive their years in sixth, seventh, and eighth grades, they began sharing frustrating experiences. One young woman recalled being asked, as a seventh grader, to write a five-page paper for her Industrial Technologies class—while learning in English class to write well-organized, descriptive paragraphs. One older man recalled his bewilderment in moving from class to class to class without being able to see any relationships among them. He commented that this lack of connection among what different teachers did was, in his experience, most problematic in English and social studies. In English, his teacher was doing a unit on poetry at one point, asking students about their knowledge of Colonial American history as a preface for discussing a particular poem. However, in social studies they were studying the "Cradle of Civilization" and the early Mesopotamian cultures. Another future teacher of math said that he decided to become a math teacher in part because he became so distressed when his science teacher in eighth grade would have to explain an algebraic process that was not due to appear in the math curriculum for several months. He said he had felt, even as a thirteen-year-old, that there should be a better way to organize the information.

These future teachers recognize several essential truths about middle schools and middle grade students. First, middle grade students are developing so rapidly in so many ways that it is difficult for them to focus on anything other than their individual needs and interests at particular points in time. They are trying to cope with all the changes brought about by puberty and by their mind's increasing ability to deal with abstractions and to do formal operational thinking. They are trying to cope with the changes involved in their movement from the comfort of the neighborhood elementary school to a more broadly based middle school. They are trying to cope with their changing relationship with their family, and with a developing sense of the world and their concern about their place in it.

Second, the fragmentation of the typical curricular structure reinforces middle grade students' sense that school is not all that important. As one twelve-year-old student of my acquaintance puts it, "When you only have to *do* English for forty-five minutes a day and nobody else cares about complete sentences and spelling and stuff, then you figure those things can't be all that important except to the English teacher. The same's true for math and the other subjects. I mean, when did any of my teachers even ask what we'd done that day in P.E. or science for that matter?" Students like this young man have recognized something that middle school educators have long argued and that is at the heart of the rationale for developing transdisciplinary, concept-based units focused on literature that speaks directly to young adolescents.

Thus, the premise of this book is that young adult literary texts, those written specifically for the young adolescent reader, can be the ideal starting point for developing concept-based, transdisciplinary units of study that reflect the needs and interests of middle level students.

## What Is Young Adult Literature?

Ken Donelson and Alleen Pace Nilsen, in *Literature for Today's Young Adults* (1993), state,

> We confess to feeling a bit pretentious when referring to a twelve- or thirteen-year-old as a young adult. However, we shy away from using the term "adolescent literature" because, as librarians have told us, "It has the ugly ring of pimples and puberty"; "It's like a conference about young adults with none present"; and "It suggests 'immature,' in a derogatory sense." . . .
>
> By "young adult literature" we mean anything that readers between the approximate ages of twelve and twenty choose to read (as opposed to what they may be coerced to read for class assignments). When we talk about "children's literature" we refer to books released by the juvenile or junior division of a publisher and intended for children from prekindergarten to about sixth grade. (6)

Contemporary young adult literature is written for and about young people from the age of eleven, when most students enter sixth grade (the grade that frequently marks the first year of middle school), through the age of eighteen, when the majority of students graduate from high school. Also, contemporary young adult literature is marketed to this audience by publishers who have come to recognize the consumer power of this age group.

Contemporary young adult literature tends to share several structural characteristics that reflect the interests of its intended readers: a young adult main character from twelve to twenty years old; one major plot, with few subplots, taking place within a fairly short time span; a limited number of characters; one major setting; and an approximate length of 125–250 pages. The language of young adult literature usually realistically echoes the language of young adults themselves.

Contemporary young adult literature reflects the complexity of the society out of which it is produced; its themes are of importance to young adults, and the issues with which the characters wrestle are of significance in our ever-changing world.

Of course, because young adult readers can be unpredictable in their reading tastes and habits, and because young adult authors—like any artists—sometimes try to push the limits of the medium in which they work, there are numerous examples of texts which violate this list of "typical" characteristics. Walter Dean Myers' *The Glory Field* (1994) covers over one hundred years of one family's history, following young representatives from each generation as they struggle to craft an identity for themselves as African Americans in a changing American society. Jerry Spinelli's *Night of the Whale* (1985), while written from a first person point of view, in fact chronicles one week in the life of a whole group of high school seniors celebrating their recent graduation and attempting to get ready for life afterward, and *Julie's Daughter* (1985) by Colby Rodowsky is told through the voices of three different narrators who speak in alternating chapters. Numerous recent titles violate the 250-page "limit," such as *The Frozen Waterfall* by Hiçyilmaz (1994), or *Monkey Tag*, by Fromm (1994).

## The Reading Interests and Abilities of Middle School Students

Samuel Johnson once wrote, "A man ought to read just as his inclination leads him, for what he reads as a task will do him little good." Teachers who agree with Johnson and who, therefore, seek to find books that their students will *want* to read, should have some familiarity with the genre of young adult literature because in young adult literature readers will find protagonists wrestling with the same developmental tasks they face themselves. The characters in young adult literary texts are concerned with developing relationships with their peers, practicing more sophisticated social skills, trying to determine an appropriate social role, adapting to their changing bodies, struggling to achieve an independent identity with their own set of values, and trying to determine how they fit into the larger societal context (Havighurst 1972). Middle school students who can find evidence that their own struggles with these concerns are validated in the pages of the texts they read are more likely to want to continue turning pages; it is their own life stories they find represented there, and they want to know how those stories might end.

Also, middle school teachers seeking to motivate their students to perceive reading as valuable should probably be familiar with research on the developmental stages of reading appreciation. Initially, young children have to learn to associate "pleasure and profit" with the printed word, according to Donelson and Nilsen (1993, 48–57). Once this connection has been made, children have the motivation to want to learn to decode texts for themselves, and they begin to learn to read, finding their own rewards for engaging in this difficult process. Margaret Early (1960) calls this stage of reading "unconscious enjoyment." Frequently children in this stage read voraciously—but read, to their parents' and teachers' dismay, the same kinds of books over and over again. Donelson and Nilsen (1993) find, however, that all of their college students who have continued to be avid readers went through stages of addiction to specific kinds of books. They postulate that "readers find comfort in knowing the characters in a book and what to expect. They develop the speed and skill that stand them in good stead when they tire of a particular kind of book" (51). By third or fourth grade, good readers develop the ability to lose themselves in a story. Time stops for readers in this stage when they are reading; all that matters is that the pages keep turning, that the story line continues to unfold.

In the second stage as outlined by Early, readers continue to accept and enjoy literature, as they did in the first stage, but they become willing to engage in efforts to enhance their own delight. According to Early, this stage of enjoyment occurs during late elementary and early middle school grades as more experienced readers begin to demand logic in their texts—logical character development and logical sequences of cause and effect in plot. Donelson and Nilsen elaborate on Early's second stage by noting that, as readers become more experienced and more cognitively sophisticated, they are able to develop a critical stance toward a book. They reject stereotypes; they want to know why things happen as they do in a story. They read to find out about themselves, hence the popularity of young adult fiction for these readers as they devour books, searching for characters who can shed some light on the process of living. Then, as their egocentrism begins to subside, senior high students become capable of "venturing beyond themselves" (Donelson and Nilsen 1993, 53), and they assess the world around them through its portrayal in literature, though they continue to search for clues about their place in that world. Carlsen (1980) calls this level of reading one of "concern for philosophical problems." Readers at this stage are interested in the interpretations and meanings of the text; they read to find out about relationships, responsibility, values, and concern for the larger world in general.

Finally, Early (1960) and others find that at the fullest level of literary appreciation, readers not only find joy in reading, but they are able to articulate the reasons for their response. As Early writes, "A sign of maturity as a human being and as a reader is that a deeper feeling for mankind replaces narrow concern for oneself. The mature reader no longer seeks only self-knowledge in literature but, with the artist, digs at the wellsprings of life." Mature readers read for aesthetic, as well as for psychological and sociological reasons. It is important to note that, unlike what is said to happen to individuals as described by other developmental stage theories, readers do not abandon one stage as they move into the next. Mature, able readers do not only read for aesthetic reasons; they read for many reasons, and they use various kinds of skills and approaches to texts depending on those reasons. They read for many reasons all at once; and sometimes they read just for the sheer delight of losing themselves in a book. At other times, their interest in the aesthetics of a text makes them participate in reading as "an extension of the creative process which produced the work of literature" in the first place.

## The Appropriateness of Young Adult Literature for Middle School Students

Carlsen (1980) makes three further generalizations about reading patterns among young adults that, as a middle school teacher, I relied on to support my use of young adult literature as the basis for transdisciplinary curricular development in the middle grades. First, he finds that young adults selecting reading material are more influenced by their chronological age than by their mental age or their school ability index. Young adults of a given age will be more likely to enjoy the same kinds of texts than the differences in their backgrounds, reading skills, and school achievements might otherwise indicate. Thus, Carlsen suggests caution in forcing able young adults to read adult literature that may be comprehensible to them on a literal level but to which they may have little emotional and psychological connection. Doing so may cause these readers to lose a sense of excitement and enthusiasm for reading and may cause them to view it as a school-based chore. A friend of mine, a gifted young woman who attended an Ivy League school, told me she stopped reading fiction as soon as she graduated from high school because her school experiences taught her to perceive novels as subjects for the analysis of times and places and emotions that held little relevance for her. She confessed that she did not read a book for pleasure for eleven years; when her first child was born, she rediscovered the wonder of books as she read to her daughter.

Our more recent understanding of reading comprehension suggests that the reader's knowledge and experiential background significantly affect ease of comprehension. Students are more likely to make sense of difficult syntax and vocabulary if they are able to connect to the text emotionally and if they are able to relate it to their world. If my friend had been asked to read novels for young adults at least some of the time during her secondary school years, perhaps she would not have turned away from reading as a leisure-time activity.

Second, some cultural influences affect the reading choices of young adults. For example, some specific differences exist between the reading tastes of adolescent males and those of females. Young women tend to read more fiction than young men, and adolescent males show little interest in paperback romance series such as the Sunset Fire books that are marketed primarily to a female audience. Teachers who assume all students will enjoy all books equally may contribute to a perception that reading is not a pleasurable activity.

Finally, Carlsen finds that young adults choose texts based on their interest in the subject matter of a book rather than on its literary merits. If the subject matter is of sufficient interest, the least able young adult reader may slog through a very difficult book. In *The New Hooked on Books*, Daniel Fader (1976) describes a young man of very limited reading skill who plowed through *The Scarlet Letter* looking for the "good parts" because he had been told it was about "a whore." After months of reading, he finished the book and said, "You know, she weren't no whore." His interest in the topic pulled him into this text that no English teacher would have assumed he could read, and Hawthorne's power as a storyteller kept him involved until, finally, his view of Hester became much more sophisticated and, at least in part, he understood what Hawthorne was trying to say about her.

Teachers who understand the developmental nature of reading appreciation recognize that their students will represent various stages of development. They also recognize, however, that young adult literature is a wonderful match for most middle grade readers for several reasons. First of all, as is true for readers at all levels, if their reading needs and interests are not met, reading becomes a chore for middle school students, and we lose them as members of the reading community, as readers who value reading as a leisure time activity.

The subject matter of young adult novels and the nature of the characters and their relationships is such that middle school students can use reading as a way to help them find out more about themselves, the world, and their relationship to it. Also, at-risk students find that the independence of the characters in young adult novels provides them with hope that they, too, can learn to cope with the problems that being an adolescent in this country carries with it.

For example, Davey, from Chris Lynch's *Gypsy Davey* (1994) lives with the knowledge that his mother abandoned him, passing him along to his older sister. Then she becomes a mother, and passes her baby along to Davey, who, at age twelve, does his best to care for the child. When his mother and sister are too mean or too depressed, and his head feels hot and jumbled inside, Davey escapes by riding and riding and riding his bike. His sister eventually leaves with a young man and the baby, leaving Davey alone and lonely, reflecting,

> Anyway soon sooner than you think probably because I'm almost a man already I'm gonna have my own find somebody who's gonna love me and we're gonna have some babies and I'm gonna love 'em like hell to pieces like nobody ever loved babies before. (179)

Like Davey, Brett, in *Yours, Brett* by Gertrude Samuels (1989) lacks a loving, stable home. She spends six years in various foster homes, all the while hoping for the love of her natural parents. Davey and Brett aren't alone in their quest for love. According to Edwards and Young (1992), at any given time, 25 percent of American children live with one parent, usually their mother, and according to Hodgkinson (1991), almost 50 percent of American children will spend some time with only one parent by the time they reach age eighteen.

Many children, also like Davey, experience emotional, physical, or sexual abuse. Edelman (1989) reports that in 1989, over 1800 children were abused daily in the United States. For some children, like Davey, the abuse is fairly noticeable. For others, like Ariel Brecht in Lynn Hall's *Flyaway* (1987), it is difficult for outsiders to believe that her seemingly perfect family harbors a man who psychologically abuses not only Ariel, but also her mother and sister.

Some abused children come from homes in which the responsible adults cannot act responsibly because of their addiction to drugs or alcohol. Gress (1992) finds that children who grow up in such environments learn to distrust the world and to cope with their mistrust either by taking total control or by totally abdicating responsibility and control for their actions.

Many children model the adult abuse of drugs and alcohol they witness. Buff Saunders in Shep Greene's *The Boy Who Drank Too Much* (1988) is an example of how a young man, torn between his own desires and the demands of an abusive, alcoholic father, turns to alcohol himself as a coping strategy; and the unnamed narrator is, as Buff's friend, also affected by the cycle of addiction.

Buff lives at home and takes the abuse of his father. Many young people who perceive themselves as unwanted and unloved leave their homes, as have the young people whose voices are heard in *Runaways* (Artenstein 1994), a collection of personal narratives by adolescents living on the streets. They are not alone in their homelessness. Artenstein reports on one 1986 study citing that in California alone anywhere between 12,700 and 128,000 children are runaways, depending on the season (viii). Adolescents living on their own are likely to experience economic difficulties, but we also know that in 1990 one child in five grew up in poverty, and Howe speculates that by 2000, one child in four will live below the poverty line. Stella Mae Willis, the child of a migrant worker in *Home Before Dark* (Bridgers 1988), and *The Contender's* Alfred Brooks (Lipsyte 1987), who comes from the ghetto, share the experiences of being poor, of having to make do, of lacking security.

In addition to abuse, divorce, poverty, and alcohol- and drug-related problems, young adults today frequently have to cope with stress, death, violence, and the risks of being sexually active—from conceiving a baby to contracting AIDS. Adolescents from minority cultures continue to endure racial prejudice, and if they are from impoverished backgrounds as well, the likelihood of their becoming at risk for school failure increases almost exponentially. Our society's mobility has accelerated to the point that one in four Americans relocates each year (Wiles and Bondi 1993, 41). Middle schoolers are most affected by this trend, because parents will frequently wait to separate or to move to an economically more inviting climate until children have finished elementary school.

The lack of stability is perhaps one of the reasons that 43 percent of all persons arrested for serious crimes—crimes of rape, murder, and robbery—are juveniles. Increasingly, young adults not only witness but participate in violent acts, join gangs that create group identities through violence, and perceive violence as a logical way to express anger and frustration. Reading novels such as Ruby's *Skin Deep* (1994), about a young man who joins a gang of Skinheads, or Henegan's *Torn Away* (1994), about a young boy growing up in Northern Ireland and enmeshed in the on-going conflicts there, may help middle school students recognize that others have faced similar situations and decisions and that alternatives to violent options are available. My point is that young adult literature provides a mirror in which middle school students can look at themselves and their world and can learn about themselves, about others, and about the nature of literature with a degree of comfort and security that other kinds of texts often fail to provide.

As a beginning teacher I was frustrated with the curriculum I was given for my gifted eighth graders. Over the course of the year, we were to trace the history of the concept *hero* by reading, first *Beowulf*, then other representative titles from various ages through the present, including sections from *La Morte D'Arthur* and other classic texts. It seemed to me even then that able or gifted students also deserve to read texts about characters to whom they can relate. In general, young adult novels present youthful protagonists dealing with family issues, peer pressures, uneasiness about the future, and concern with immediate decisions; gifted students are no different from their peers in terms of their need to wrestle with such problems, and they, too, can find themselves in the pages of many young adult texts.

Reading C. S. Adler's *Kiss the Clown* (1986)—about a bright but severely dyslexic young man whose emotional problems cause him suffering in school—or Naylor's *Send No Blessings* (1990)—about an intelligent and diligent young woman who has trouble academically in part because of her impoverished background and lack of parental support—may prove beneficial for talented students who are, themselves, having difficulties fitting into the world of school. Similarly, *Midnight Hour Encores* by Bruce Brooks (1986), about a gifted musician and her father, or *In Summer Light* by Zibby Oneal (1985), about a young artist and her efforts to be true to her gifts, may serve the gifted adolescent well.

Because young adult literature provides the middle school student with easy access into the story, teachers can employ young adult titles as the basis for helping students appreciate literature as art and understand how it is crafted. Although experts in the field of young adult literature no longer use the term "junior novel" because of its pejorative connotations, the arguments made by Robert Small almost twenty years ago in "The Junior Novel and the Art of Literature" (1977) still hold:

> [T]he art is there, and we are the ones to teach about it. . . . One thing simplicity of form does is to force us to get off our podiums and drop the pose of expert. How can we maintain our role of truth-giver when many of our students are already beginning to find the nature of the literary art for themselves? . . . As a healthy catharsis for us all, a study of the art of the junior novel may lead us to realize that students are not so dumb about literature, that they can understand—with only a little help from us—the workings of things like plot and setting and theme.

He continues,

> The well-written junior novel, in contrast [to the adult novel], invites, welcomes students to meet it as equals. They can become real authorities on the literary craft of books like *Johnny May* (Brascum) or *A Hero Ain't Nothin' but a Sandwich* (Childress). They can establish a critical relationship to *Fair Day, and Another Step Begun* (Lyle) or *Z for Zachariah* (O'Brien). (57)

Finally, because young adult literature does invite adolescent readers in, rather than keeping them at an emotional distance, they can begin to understand the transactional nature of the reading act. Theorists from Iser to Rosenblatt to Probst argue that we cannot be objective about a literary work. Instead of studying "the" interpretation of a text, Iser (1974) advocates using texts to help readers resolve tensions and reconsider concepts. Literature presents its readers with new perceptions and invites them to use their imaginations to extend the story in diverse ways. Iser writes,

> If the reader were given the whole story, and there were nothing left for him to do, then his imagination would never enter the field, the result would be the boredom which inevitably arises when everything is cut and dried before us. A literary text must therefore be conceived in such a way that it will engage the reader's imagination in the task of working things out for himself, for reading is only a pleasure when it is active and creative. (275)

Probst (1986), applying what Iser says to adolescent readers, notes that they need literature that will awaken them to differences, and will compel them to engage with the text creatively:

> Adolescent readers are most likely to want to pursue that quest if the literature they encounter deals with issues that are significant to them. Thus good adolescent literature is especially useful in the English classroom. Although literature for adolescents may not have the substance of the literature traditionally at the core of the high school curriculum, it has the virtue of addressing itself to matters in which students are likely to take an interest and thus to stimulate the effort to "actualize," or to make meaning out of the text. (35)

Listen to Harper from Kathryn Lasky's *Memoirs of a Bookbat* (1994) describe the delicious feelings she has when reading a book, feelings we want all our students to have about literature:

> Just that afternoon at the library storytime, Nancy had read a beautiful poem about a baby bat being born. It described bats' "sharp ears, their sharp teeth, their quick sharp faces." It told how they soared and looped through the night, how they listened by sending out what the poetry called "shining needlepoints of sound." Bats live by hearing. I realized, standing in front of Nettie right then, that when I read I am like a bat soaring and swooping through the night, skimming across the treetops to find my way through the densest forest in the darkest night. I listen to the shining needlepoints of sound in every book I read. I am no bookworm. I am the bookbat. (31–32)

Teachers who understand the developmental nature of reading appreciation and who want to provide opportunities for all adolescents to feel the pleasure of being "bookbats" should consider the power of young adult literature as a tool in their quest to do so.

## Young Adult Literature and Concept-Based Transdisciplinary Units in the Middle School

Edward Fiske (1991) describes the traditional, liberal arts model of curriculum—separating disciplines into compartments to be learned independently of each other—as being inconsistent with the demands of today's society. Fiske says this model is

> incompatible with the new demand for thinking and problem-solving skills. . . . Today's information society requires more than the accumulation of knowledge and recitation of facts. . . . The most important attribute that schools can give students is the ability to learn on their own. (65)

Literature written specifically for young adults can provide a scaffold for transdisciplinary study, a curricular model more in keeping with the demands outlined by Fiske, because of its inherent attention to the issues and concerns central to the drama of adolescence, concerns which cross traditional curricular content boundaries. Stevens (1993) argues that concept-based transdisciplinary units should be grounded in literary texts because of the universal themes explored in literature that are common to the human condition, and she documents how involvement in such units increases students' active participation, collaboration, and personal investment in the learning process. Basically, a young adult text can provide "the specific illustrative context within which the theme is explored and developed" (Grady 1994, 6).

At some point, students may either need or desire a discipline-based approach to learning and curriculum. Different academic disciplines do have a certain amount of integrity. The literary scholar's way of looking at the world or of attacking a problem may be quite different from that of the mathematician or the economist or physicist, and there are times when it is useful to frame a problem from a particular point of reference or to study data using the tools of a particular discipline. However, even on university campuses, the boundary lines between traditional academic disciplines are growing increasingly blurry. And, in general, as James Beane (1990) notes, forced maintenance of content-area boundaries is "alien to life."

Although many theorists use the term *interdisciplinary* to describe the kind of integrated curricular model appropriate for middle school students, *transdisciplinary—trans* meaning, of course, *across*—better captures the idea of transcending traditional content-area boundaries, of exploring genuine problems from multiple perspectives without concern for content-area divisions (Tchudi 1991; Drake 1993). On the other hand, an *interdisciplinary* approach tends to be used to describe the situation that exists when teachers of different content areas explore how a given theme plays out within the confines of their traditional disciplines. *Transdisciplinary* better describes what *The Middle School Interdisciplinary Performance-Based Team Activities* bulletin of Baltimore County Public Schools calls for when it says, "This approach helps students discover the natural connections and linkages among subject areas in order to acquire the skills and knowledge which transcend the more narrowly-defined learning objectives in any one discipline" (1).

For middle grade students, the transdisciplinary approach provides opportunities to focus on their personal concerns in the context of larger social issues and to use the tools of several disciplines all at once in exploration of a specific theme, thus increasing the possibility that they will see the relevance of school in their lives. Additionally, transdisciplinary units frequently provide opportunities for students to learn more about themselves and others while also learning important content and skills. This attribute relates directly to what is known about the younger adolescent's cognitive and emotional/social development and to what we know about the appeal of young adult literature to this group of readers. As Gardner (1994) notes, true transdisciplinary work "can only be legitimately attempted if one has already mastered at least a portion of specific disciplines" (17). By the time students reach middle school, they should have the tools—derived from various content fields—needed for this kind of work, and they should be able to use these tools in ways that help them see the relevance of their education. By using their skills and prior knowledge in the exploration of concepts important to them, middle school students can experience a sense of relevancy that my students craved—and lacked—in their schooling.

James Beane (1990), in *A Middle School Curriculum: From Rhetoric to Reality*, provides the following list of possible curricular themes that intersect with the young adolescent's personal and increasingly important social concerns: transitions, identities, interdependence, wellness, social structures, independence, conflict resolution, commercialism, justice, caring, institutions. In 1992, Beane described the translation of this vision of transdisciplinary curricular organization into reality at Marquette Middle School in Madison, Wisconsin, where the organizing principle is that of adolescents questioning themselves and their world and participating in the curricular planning. In "The

Search for a Middle School Curriculum" (1993b), he further demonstrates the power of a transdisciplinary, concept-based curricular organization through three case studies, as does Hall (1993) in a study of Meyer Middle School in River Falls, Wisconsin. Research by Hough (1994), on the effects of participating in a transdisciplinary unit on patterns, and by Peters (1985), on a global education unit, also provides evidence that students are excited about and interested in studying concepts in this fashion.

There is also some research to suggest that middle school curricula organized around such units can help at-risk youth become more likely to succeed academically. For instance, the Middle School Efficacy Program in Detroit, Michigan described by Syropoulos (1990) has replaced traditional units with units on concepts such as motivation, taking moderate academic risks, envisioning positive futures, setting realistic goals, and working cooperatively. Experimental groups have exceeded control groups in areas such as citizenship, school attitudes, reading, math, and attendance in such programs. Why? Such programs are designed first of all to attend to middle school students' needs, helping them develop a sense of security in the school and in the classroom. Then, such programs help students build on that sense of security to feel a sense of belonging, which in turn helps them to foster their sense of self-esteem, a crucial step in working toward self-fulfillment according to Maslow (1970). McCarty et al. (1991) describe similar results achieved through the use of transdisciplinary approach emphasizing open-ended questions, inductive/analytic reasoning, and student verbalization for Navajo students in a Navajo Studies program. Other examples of such projects include the Stanford Accelerated Schools Project, described by Hopfenberg, Levin, Meister, and Rogers (1990), The Edna McConnell Clark Foundation's Program for Disadvantaged Youth (Mizell and Gonzalez 1991), and individual school district efforts, such as The Syracuse Stay in School Partnership Project (Meyer, Harootunian, and William 1991), the Ysleta Middle School of El Paso's STAR Project (George and Alexander 1993), and the primarily Hispanic Pajaro Middle School in California (Garcia 1990).

Additionally, Smith and Johnson (1993) document the positive results their students achieved in both attitude and content development when they led a group of seventh graders in designing and implementing a unit on death and dying, centered about literary texts and journal writing activities. And Lawton's 1994 study of test results from 1950 to the present of over 15,000 Maine students showed that those who experienced a transdisciplinary middle school curriculum outscored their peers enrolled in a curriculum organized around individual disciplines by an average of 58 points.

George and Alexander in *The Exemplary Middle School* (1993) state,

The point of greatest significance is that the middle school must be uniquely planned, staffed, and operated to provide a program that is truly focused on the rapidly moving and changing learners in transition from childhood to adolescence. . . . The chief implication of our knowledge about middle school learners is that they need a school focused sharply on their needs. (21)

How do transdisciplinary units relate to the unique needs of middle school students? Consider, for example, a unit titled "Transitions." Students concerned about, and living through, the agony of the transition from childhood to adulthood, can explore transition as a concept as it relates to the world beyond themselves. As they seek to answer questions such as "What does it mean to be 'in transition'?" or "What processes are involved in making a transition?" they can investigate the examples listed in the following chart of how transitions are found in all aspects of life. (In order to demonstrate that content-area knowledge as traditionally defined can be presented through transdisciplinary units, this chart is organized by traditional disciplines, although, in a truly transdisciplinary approach, all teachers on a team, working together, would deal with these examples as the overarching questions about personal changes and changes in the world around us are answered.)

1. *Science:* What happens to the caterpillar during the transitional chrysalis period before it emerges as a butterfly? What transitions does wood undergo as it becomes charcoal?

2. *Math:* What happens to the formula governing our understanding of two dimensional figures if these figures are transformed into their three dimensional counterparts?

3. *History:* How can the colonial period in American history be characterized as a time of transition from dependence to independence? How is the current state of affairs in South Africa indicative of transition as the people there struggle to find their way into new ways of living together?

4. *Language and writing:* What happens to verb forms as a writer makes a transition from personal journal writing in the present tense to crafted narration in the past tense? What are "transitions" in an essay?

5. *Health:* How is adolescence a transitional period? How can individuals best cope with the stresses associated with moving through transitions?

6. *Art:* In looking at the body of work by Picasso (or any artist who changed his/her style or way of seeing and expressing him/herself over time), which paintings or other pieces of art show evidence

that he was in a transitional mode, moving from one period of his life and work into another?

7. *Geography/geology:* What does it mean to say that a culture is in transition? If we are currently moving from one geological time period into another, what are the indicators that this is the case, and what kind of movement is happening around us?

Engaging in the study of "transition" as a naturally occurring phenomenon that has implications for all parts of life should provide a sense of comfort for younger adolescents caught up in difficult transitions of their own, adolescents who, like Walker, from Chris Crutcher's *Stotan!* (1986), are discovering

> We're brought up to think that the good guys are rewarded and the bad guys are punished; but upon close scrutiny, that assumption vanishes into thin air.... And who are the bad guys anyway? .... All questions; no answers. . . . But I guess I have learned a few things. I've learned that asking "why" is more often than not a waste of time; that it's much more important just to know what is so. (181–82)

I have learned that transdisciplinary units focused on literature about adolescents experiencing anxiety and tension can help students realize they are not alone in their struggles to cope with the tumultuous state of their bodies and their fluctuating reasoning capabilities. Having a literary text at the heart of their transdisciplinary work also provides students still not all that adept at abstract thought with a concrete context for exploring abstract concepts. And working with peers to solve real-life puzzles growing out of their reading can help them perceive themselves as part of a group, which is consistent with a fundamental mission of schools: "to produce people capable of living with some degree of responsibility and care for one another" (Oliner 1986, 404). In short, such units provide a sense of solace for young adults because they aid abstract thought and provide a context for being part of a larger whole.

The themes developed through literature transcend traditional content-area boundaries and provide a natural framework for unifying the curriculum. When young adult readers connect with and come to care about a character in a book, *they* want to know more about that character. This desire to enter into the world of the text fosters inquiry, and inquiry-based teaching is rather different from the often-employed "discovery learning" approach. Teachers who describe their pedagogical strategies as "discovery" oriented often know the goal; they know what it is they want the students to discover, and they use experimental, collaborative, and exploratory techniques to guide students to those predetermined "discoveries."

True inquiry teaching, on the other hand, assumes a more balanced partnership between teacher and students in the learning process; students participate in determining what it is they want to investigate and how they want to do so. They may want to know more about the time and place in which the story takes place; they may want to try to solve problems the characters encounter; they may want to learn more about other works by the same author; they may want to track down references and allusions found within the text; they may want to investigate references to historical events, scientific terms, or economic theories embedded in the context of the unfolding narrative (Harste and Short 1995).

As Robert Coles (1989) describes in *The Call of Stories: Teaching and the Moral Imagination*, story is a powerful way of knowing because it provides a context for solving real problems and thus for learning; in short, it provides the opportunities and motivation for students to learn on their own that educators such as Fiske demand. Similarly, Hicks and Austin (1994), Smith and Johnson (1993), Nevin (1992), and Cooter (1989) describe the benefits of putting literature at the heart of transdisciplinary curriculum planning because narrative texts allow students to identify and assimilate different worldviews and more complex knowledge.

Lauritzen and Jaeger (1994) evaluated the effects of engagement in transdisciplinary study centered on a narrative text for future elementary school teachers. They used historical vignettes such as Hawthorne's "The Pine Tree Shillings" in *Stories of Our Country* (1887) and historical fiction for young adults such as Katherine Lasky's *The Bone Wars* (1988). They summarize their project by stating,

> Transdisciplinary curriculum is filled with opportunities for bringing context and meaning to the goals of education. Instead of a synthetic unit arranged around a process or topic, exploration of real problems places the focus on application of skills and knowledge. Students develop an appreciation and respect for the language and culture of others as they read and enjoy the literature of Hawthorne or the diaries of the Oregon Trail emigrants. They are better able to recognize when language is being used to manipulate and coerce as they discover the role of propagandizing done in the name of Manifest Destiny or the seemingly simple matter of dating a coin. Practicing the process of communication becomes a natural adjunct of finding out about the places, people and events of the Oregon Trail or colonial Massachusetts. Linking specific language arts goals to the larger goals embraced by the integrated nature of the curriculum affords authentic opportunity for learning. (586)

The future teachers described by these authors are eloquent in their reflections upon why the transdisciplinary, narrative framework experience was so powerful: Because young adult literature is more accessible to young adolescent readers, because they understand and relate to the emotional life of characters experiencing the same transition from childhood to adulthood that they, as readers, are going through, young adult literature is the ideal source of narrative for developing concept-based transdisciplinary units.

Almost any of the concepts used as the basis for transdisciplinary planning can be related to significant "categories of concern" (Donelson and Nilsen 1993) found in young adult literature as well as to the tasks adolescents must complete (Havighurst 1972) in order to progress developmentally (Figure 1–1). In Naidoo's *Chain of Fire* (1990), for example, two teenagers, Naledi and Taolo, residents of the South African village of Bophelong, are forced to go with their families to a barren patch of country the government has said will be their "homeland." As they struggle to deal with the difficulties of surviving in this harsh environment and maintaining their identity and spirit in the face of the realities of apartheid, they learn the importance of cooperation, and they learn that they have to fight for their rights because nobody else will fight for them. They eventually help to lead a resistance movement, gaining in the process an increased sense of their values, of their own significance in the larger social order, and of who they are as individuals within their culture and within their country. They have to find ways to communicate over time and space, and juggle the demands of tradition and justice. In short, their story illustrates most of the concepts considered useful for initiating transdisciplinary study.

Appendix B demonstrates possibilities for relating young adult literary texts to concepts considered useful and appropriate for middle school students. That list is merely a starting point, designed to indicate the richness of young adult literature as a source and focal point when planning transdisciplinary units. The list includes titles that long have been incorporated into American middle school curricula and that lend themselves to whole-group instruction and study, such as *Roll of Thunder, Hear My Cry* (Taylor 1976), or *The Pigman* (Zindel 1969), *The Chocolate War* (Cormier 1974), and *The Outsiders* (Hinton 1967), and newer titles, such as *Make Lemonade* (Wolff 1993), *Toning the Sweep* (Johnson 1993), or *Chain of Fire* (Naidoo 1990), that are challenging and rich enough to deserve study by an entire class.

The list also includes titles more appropriate for independent reading when freely chosen by students introduced to them through book talks about titles that deal with a particular thematic concept, such as Danziger's *The Cat Ate My Gymsuit* (1974) or Johnston's *The Image Game* (1994). It attempts, too, to indicate that titles reflecting a

Figure 1–1

## Categories of Adolescent Concern, Related Concepts, and Related Developmental Tasks

1. FAMILY RELATIONSHIPS
   Related Concepts: courage, communication, change, structure, survival, balance, culture, truth, progress, environments, freedom, frontiers, justice, power, tradition, community, expression, proof, beginnings, relationships, independence, immigration, boundaries, color, sources, cycles, patterns, time, adaptation, exploration, conflict, symbols, forces, honor, origins, confrontation, space, beliefs, rights, behavior, homes.
   Related Developmental Tasks: achieving a proper masculine or feminine role; achieving emotional independence from parents and other adults; acquiring a personal ideology or value system; achieving social responsibility.

2. FRIENDS AND SOCIETY
   Related Concepts: courage, communication, change, structure, survival, balance, cultures, truth, energy, progress, environments, war, freedom, frontiers, justice, power, tradition, community, expression, proof, design, trends, style, beginnings, relationships, independence, immigration, influences, color, boundaries, sources, cycles, patterns, time, adaptations, exploration, extinction, conflict, symbols, forces, origins, confrontation, space, beliefs, rights, behavior, homes.
   Related Developmental Tasks: achieving new and more mature relations with age-mates; achieving a proper masculine or feminine social role; achieving emotional independence and using the body effectively; preparing for marriage and family; preparing for an economic career; acquiring personal ideology or value system; achieving social responsibility.

3. RACIAL, ETHNIC, AND CLASS RELATIONSHIPS
   Related Concepts: courage, communication, change, structure, survival, balance, culture, truth, energy, progress, environments, war, freedom, frontiers, justice, power, tradition, community, expression, proof, trends, style, beginnings, relationships, independence, immigration, influences, color, boundaries, sources, cycles, patterns, time, adaptations, exploration, extinction, conflict, symbols, forces, honor, origins, space, beliefs, rights, behavior, homes.
   Related Developmental Tasks: achieving new and more mature relations with age-mates; achieving a proper masculine or feminine social role; achieving emotional independence from parents and other adults; preparing for marriage and family; preparing for

continued

an economic career; acquiring a personal ideology or value system; achieving social responsibility.

4. BODY AND SELF
Related Concepts: courage, communication, change, structure, survival, balance, truth, culture, energy, progress, environment, war, freedom, power, tradition, community, expression, proof, design, style, beginnings, relationships, independence, influences, color, boundaries, sources, cycles, patterns, time, adaptation, extinction, conflict, symbols, forces, honor, origins, confrontation, space, beliefs, rights, behavior, homes.
Related Developmental Tasks: achieving new and more mature relations with age-mates; achieving a proper masculine or feminine social role; adapting to physical changes and using the body effectively; preparing for marriage and family; acquiring a personal ideology or value system; achieving social responsibility.

5. SEXUAL RELATIONSHIPS
Related Concepts: courage, communication, change, structure, survival, balance, culture, truth, environment, freedom, war, frontiers, justice, power, tradition, community, expression, proof, trends, style, beginnings, relationships, independence, influences, color, boundaries, patterns, time, adaptation, exploration, extinction, conflict, symbols, forces, honor, origins, confrontation, space, beliefs, rights, behavior, homes.
Related Developmental Tasks: achieving new and more mature relations with age-mates; achieving a proper masculine or feminine social role; adapting to physical changes and using the body effectively; achieving emotional independence from parents and other adults; preparing for marriage and a family; acquiring a personal ideology or value system.

variety of cultural perspectives and from a variety of genres are available for more and less sophisticated readers, so that there should be a way for teachers to find books suited to all their students' reading needs and interests that relate to curricular demands.

One caution, however: Because young adult literature at its best realistically portrays the life and concerns of adolescents, teachers will have to read the books to determine whether or not the community—parents, leaders of community institutions—in which an individual title is to be used will perceive its value and will not protest its presence on the bookshelf. For instance, titles such as Rylant's *A Fine White Dust* (1989) and Myers' *Somewhere in the Darkness* (1992) and

*Scorpions* (1988) have both the thematic content and the literary merit required for in-common reading, but because of the controversial subject matters and realistic language, these books may not be appropriate for whole class study in some school districts. Also, some of the titles, such as Filipovic's *Zlata's Diary* (1994), Dickinson's *Shadow of a Hero* (1994) or Voigt's *Orfe* (1992), may demand significant background knowledge—of other times, places, or content-areas—before the events described will be understood by adolescent readers. Additional resources useful in finding out about young adult titles are provided in Appendix B.

## Through What Process Can These Concepts and Texts Be Developed into Transdisciplinary Units?

The list of concepts and related texts presented in Appendix B illustrates how almost any transdisciplinary theme can be explored through literature. Sample units focused on specific works will follow in the coming chapters. These units have been developed by following a process that teachers of all age groups can use when attempting to plan for their particular students. The thinking involved in generating such units can be guided by answering the following questions:

1. *What topics and concepts are of interest to my students?* (I find it useful to brainstorm responses to this question, using the lists of concepts provided elsewhere in this text, interest surveys completed by students, observation, curriculum guides, etc.) Are these concepts related to their developmental needs and interests?

2. *What literary texts relate to the concept and are of interest to students with diverse reading interests and abilities?* (Consider such criteria as the quality of the writing, the level of emotional involvement possible for the readers to achieve, the lack of stereotyping, the accuracy of details. As Lauritzen and Jaeger (1994) say, such texts "must compel the reader primarily as a narrative and [only] then as a source of curriculum.")

3. *What skills do students need to practice? To learn?* (I have derived answers to this question from curriculum guides, from observation, parents, the students themselves, and, possibly, the mandates imposed by standardized testing systems.)

4. *What do students need to know and what is of interest to them?* (Again, the answers will derive from multiple sources.)

5. *Do the topics and concepts that are generated from question 1 and that meet the criteria implied in questions 2 and 3 allow for transdisciplinary study?*

**6.** *Do the topics and concepts generated from number one and that meet the criteria implied in questions two and three allow for exploration of multicultural perspectives?*

As each question is answered, cross out topics/concepts that need to be eliminated. Of the topics/concepts left on the list, make choices for unit planning keeping in mind the following questions:

**1.** *Do students have the prerequisite skills and content knowledge needed to adequately explore the concept?* (If the answer to this question is no, consider whether or not it is practical, given other curricular demands, to help the students reach the necessary prerequisites, or whether a new topic/concept should be selected.)

**2.** *Are there any special resources needed if students are to adequately engage in the study of the concept?* (Identify resources available within the school and outside of school to which, ideally, you would like to have access. Consider the practical issues of availability and identify those that are necessary but not available; if there are too many of these resources on your list, implementing your unit may not be feasible.)

**3.** *Will both male and female students of varying learning styles and with varying special needs be able to succeed in the study of the concept?*

Generate a list of questions that both the students and you as teacher may want to answer as the unit unfolds. Check the list to ensure that there are items that allow students to reflect on themselves, their relationships with others and with their world, and their relationships with the text. Check the list to ensure that there are transdisciplinary questions and questions that allow for a focus on the issue from content-area perspectives as well. For instance, the Tucson Unified School District identifies "Change" as a major theme and outlines, in the curriculum guide, the following key questions for teachers to explore with students:

**1.** Sample unit question: Who/what initiates change?

**2.** Sample focusing question for generating discipline-based problems: What roles do "equilibrium," and "cause and effect" play in change?

**3.** Sample disciplinary problems related to item 2:

*Math, Grades 6–8:* Design a computer program to understand and manipulate variables.

*Science, Grades 6–8:* Explore changes that are required to achieve equilibrium, such as shifting plates and earthquakes, salt water and osmosis.

*Social studies, Grades 6–8:* Examine cultural, economic, and technological changes associated with the coming of the railroad to Tucson.

*Language arts:* Examine the dynamic role of variables in change using Ray Bradbury's "The Sound of Thunder."

**4.** Sample transdisciplinary unit for grades 6–8:

Cycles: Examine the components and patterns of cyclical change (e.g., water or carbon cycles; cycles of the rise and fall of civilizations). Examine the worldview of Native American cultures (e.g., the emphasis on the number four as related to seasons; on the life cycle; on the significance for humans of the round shape in nature, etc.) [vanAllen 1994].

Several young adult novels come immediately to mind as useful keystones for this unit on "Change." In addition to those described under "Change" in Appendix B, the ecological mysteries of Jean Craighead George would provide the stimulus for much discussion and inquiry. In *The Fire Bug Connection* (1995), for instance, Maggie is eager to watch her fire bugs go through the last stage of metamorphosis and become mature adults. But most of the bugs in her collection seem to be unable to do so. These "Peter Pans" get larger and larger and finally "pop" and die, without ever being able to reproduce or fly. As Maggie and her computer whiz friend Mitch track down the environmental clues to this "murder," they find out about golden digger wasps, global warming, bats, acid rain, and environmental change in general; additionally, they learn about the changing nature of personal relationships and about the ways in which individual perceptions of the world change with time and experience. Thus, readers' concept of "change" can be broadened through reading and exploring issues derived from this fast-paced text. As they investigate the meaning of "change" from multiple perspectives, students' understanding of the concept becomes multifaceted. Like a diamond that shines more intensely and brilliantly the more faces it has, the meaning of "change" in all aspects of their lives intensifies for students as they study this concept, constantly going back to the text for grounding.

As the unit concept unfolds, other questions will arise. What kinds of activities are appropriate for the particular students in the class? Which are feasible given the reality of the resources, time, and context in which the unit will be taught? Which are useful given the desired outcomes of the unit, and are consistent with the teacher's personality, strengths, and philosophy?

In answering such questions, I have found it helpful to use a chart similar to that in Figure 1–2. Also, many curriculum specialists use

**Figure 1–2**

---

Planning Process Chart for Transdisciplinary Study
Centered on Young Adult Literature

1. Concept

2. Related Developmental Tasks/Concerns for Age Group
   (females and males)

3. Related Literary Texts

4. Required Resources

5. Prerequisite Skills/Content (from all disciplines)

6. Related Skills/Content to Be Addressed (from all
   disciplines)

7. Relationship to Curricularly Mandated Goals (and other
   mandates for program outcomes)

8. Related Disciplinary Questions

9. Transdisciplinary Questions

10. Multicultural Perspectives to Be Included

11. Required Considerations for Students with Special Needs

12. Related Activities

---

"webs" or "concept maps" as a way to plan for the study of a concept from multiple disciplinary perspectives. An example is provided in Figure 1–3.

Ross (1987) points out the problematic nature of portraying an inquiry-based curriculum in a step-by-step manner. Such a reflective, inquiry-oriented planning process that crosses discipline boundaries and that is grounded in text is more suited, on paper, to strategies such as webbing and brainstorming. The questions outlined above are meant as guidelines rather than as mandates, and there is no need to

Figure 1-3

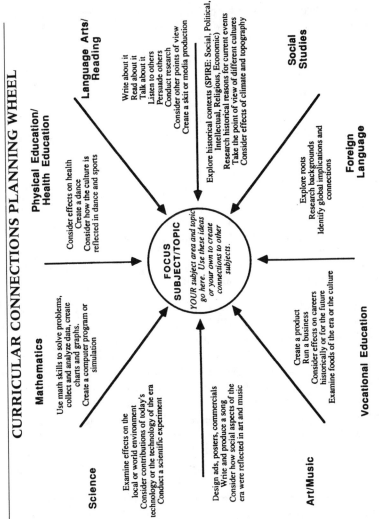

## CURRICULAR CONNECTIONS PLANNING WHEEL

**FOCUS SUBJECT/TOPIC**

*YOUR subject area and topic go here. Use these ideas or your own to create connections to other subjects.*

**Language Arts/ Reading**

Write about it
Read about it
Talk about it
Listen to others
Persuade others
Conduct research
Consider other points of view
Create a skit or media production

**Physical Education/ Health Education**

Consider effects on health
Create a dance
Consider how the culture is reflected in dance and sports

**Social Studies**

Explore historical contexts (SPIRE: Social, Political, Intellectual, Religious, Economic)
Research historical reasons for current events
Take the point of view of different cultures
Consider effects of climate and topography

**Mathematics**

Use math skills to solve problems, collect and analyze data, create charts and graphs.
Create a computer program or simulation

**Foreign Language**

Explore roots
Research backgrounds
Identify global implications and connections

**Science**

Examine effects on the local or world environment
Consider contributions of today's technology or the technology of the era
Conduct a scientific experiment

**Art/Music**

Design ads, posters, commercials
Write and produce a song
Consider how social aspects of the era were reflected in art and music

**Vocational Education**

Create a product
Run a business
Consider effects on careers historically or for the future
Examine foods of the era or the culture

consider them in the particular order in which they are listed. Michaelis (1973) and Manning et al. (1994) provide profiles of teachers engaged in planning and organizing transdisciplinary units; it has been beneficial for me to read the narrative descriptions of their thought processes, and I would recommend them to any teacher embarking on the road to creating a transdisciplinary program.

## Conclusion

A 1992 document, *English Language Arts* (1992), published by the Oregon Department of Education describes the state of English language arts education envisioned for the year 2000. In this vision of the ideal language arts environment,

> The learner is deeply engaged and committed to the process of literacy as the primary means for moving securely into an ever-expanding and exciting world of opportunities. . . . [T]he learner is able to read, write, speak, and listen critically; to solve problems by exercising his or her own judgement; to enjoy and interpret literature from many times and cultures; and to develop those new skills and attitudes that encourage life-long learning.

The more positive experiences students have with books as readers, the more likely it is they will continue to engage in literary encounters throughout their lives. Through encounters with literature readers expand their worlds, learn about other places and times, and develop tolerance for diverse points of view. They begin to recognize the difficulties inherent in generalizing from one person's story, rooted as it is in a particular context. Readers learn about their own cultural heritage and that of others, they experience vicariously the joys and frustrations others have experienced before them and may find comfort in recognizing that they are not alone in their struggles, or they may even find through their reading experiences the clue that will help them solve a puzzle in their own lives.

In general, reading, when done well, can almost always provide the basis for transdisciplinary learning. For example, one young man wrote, after reading a young adult novel from the former Soviet Union and then evaluating the ways in which his literary experience changed his stereotypes,

> I learned that public opinion or TV is definitely wrong sometimes. I know/think/believe that Russian students are just like us. I thought they would be all snobs in uniforms. . . . I found out I was wrong. They are just regular kids. (Stover with Karr 1990, 53)

This young man's reading led him to consider the role of television in modern life, led him to rethink his stereotypes and how they are formed, and led him into lots of additional research about topics as varied as carrier pigeons, World War II, and the differences between U.S. and Russian educational systems. The key point is that without the connection to and affection he felt for the young male protagonist of the book *Shadows Across the Sun* by Albert Likhanov (1983), this young man would not have been motivated to investigate any of these concepts.

The units in the next three chapters are presented as invitations, in the forms of models, for teachers to foster their ability to see transdisciplinary connections, to develop their motivation to read widely, to explore the relationship between the content of a story and the writer's craft in presenting it, and to create a community of readers sharing significant reading and learning experiences.

# Works Cited

Baltimore County Public Schools. N. d. *The Middle School Interdisciplinary Performance-Based Team Activities*. Towson, MD: Baltimore County Public Schools.

Beane, James. 1990. *A Middle School Curriculum: From Rhetoric to Reality*. Columbus, OH: National Middle School Association.

————. 1992. "Integrated Curriculum in the Middle School." ERIC Document ED351095.

————. 1993a. "Problems and Possibilities for an Integrative Curriculum." *Middle School Journal* 25(1): 18–23.

————. 1993b. "The Search for a Middle School Curriculum." *School Administrator* 50(3): 8–14.

Bradbury, Ray. 1959. "The Sound of Thunder." *Twice Twenty-Two*. New York: Doubleday.

Carlsen, G. Robert. 1980. *Books and the Teenage Reader*. 2d rev. ed. New York: Harper and Row.

Coles, Robert. 1989. *The Call of Stories: Teaching and the Moral Imagination*. Boston: Houghton Mifflin.

Cooter, Robert B. 1989. "Thematic Units for Middle School: An Honorable Seduction." *Journal of Reading* 32(8): 76–81.

Donelson, Ken, and Alleen Pace Nilsen. 1993. *Literature for Today's Young Adults*. 4th ed. New York: HarperCollins College Publishers.

Drake, Susan M. 1993. *Planning Integrated Curriculum: The Call to Adventure*. Alexandria, VA: Association for Supervision and Curriculum Development.

Early, Margaret. 1960. "Stages of Growth in Literary Appreciation." *English Journal* 49(3): 161–67.

Edelman, M. W. 1989. "Defending America's Children." *Educational Leadership* 46(8): 77.

Edwards, P. A., and L. S. J. Young. 1992. "Beyond Parents: Family, Community and School Involvement." *Phi Delta Kappan* 74(1): 72.

*English Language Arts*. 1992. Salem, OR: Oregon Department of Education.

Fader, Daniel. 1976. *The New Hooked on Books*. New York: Berkley Medallion Books.

Fiske, Edward. 1991. *Smart Kids*. New York: Simon and Schuster.

Garcia, Eugene E. 1991. "An Analysis of Literacy Enhancement for Middle School Hispanic Students Through Curriculum Integration." Paper presented at the 40th Annual Meeting of the National Reading Conference, Miami, FL, November–December. ERIC Document ED331008.

Gardner, H., and V. Boix-Mansilla. 1994. "Teaching for Understanding—Within and Across Disciplines." *Educational Leadership* 51(5): 14–18.

George, Paul S., and William M. Alexander. 1993. *The Exemplary Middle School*. New York: Holt, Rinehart, and Winston.

Grady, Joan B. 1994. "Interdisciplinary Curriculum Development." Paper presented at the 49th annual Conference of the Association for Supervision and Curriculum Development, Chicago, IL. ERIC Document ED373903.

Gress, J. R. 1992. "Family Substance Abuse and Teacher Education." *Action in Teacher Education* 14(3): 20.

Hall, Patricia H. 1993. "Focus on Meyer Middle School." *Schools in the Middle* 3(2): 49–51.

Harste, Jerome, and Kathy Short. 1995. "Inquiry, Theme Cycles, and Interdisciplinary Teaching." Presentation made at the National Council of Teachers of English Spring Conference, Minneapolis, March.

Havighurst, Robert. 1972. *Developmental Tasks and Education*. New York: David McKay.

Hicks, Karen, and Jordan Austin. 1994. "Experiencing the Legal System: Fairy Tales for Fifth Graders." *Social Studies* 85(1): 39–43.

Hodgkinson, H. 1991. "Reform Versus Reality." *Phi Delta Kappan* 73(1): 9.

Hopfenberg, W., H. Levin, G. Meister, and J. Rogers. 1990. *Toward Accelerated Middle School*. Stanford, CA: Stanford University School of Education.

Hough, David L. 1994. "Patterns: A Study of the Effects of Integrated Curricula on Young Adolescent's Problem-Solving Ability." Paper presented at the Annual Meeting of the American Educational Research Association, New Orleans, Louisiana, April 4–8.

Iser, Wolfgang. 1974. *The Implied Reader: Patterns of Communication in Prose Fiction from Bunyan to Beckett*. Baltimore: Johns Hopkins University Press.

Lauritzen, Carol, and Michael Jaeger. 1994. "Language Arts Teacher Education Within a Transdisciplinary Curriculum." *Language Arts* 71(8): 581–87.

Lawton, Ed. 1994. "Integrating the Curriculum: A Slow but Positive Process." *Schools in the Middle* 4(2): 27–30.

Manning, Maryann, et al. 1994. *Theme Immersion: Inquiry-Based Curriculum in Elementary and Middle Schools.* ERIC Document ED370100.

Maslow, Abraham. 1970. *Motivation and Personality.* 2d ed. New York: Harper and Row.

McCarty, T. L., et al. 1991. "Classroom Inquiry and Navajo Learning Styles: A Call for Reassessment." *Anthropology and Education Quarterly* 22(1): 42–59.

Meyer, L., B. Harootunian, and D. William. 1991. "Inclusive Middle Schooling Practices: Shifting from Deficit to Support Models." Paper presented at the American Educational Research Association Conference, Chicago, Illinois. April. ERIC Document ED332355.

Michaelis, John U. 1973. *Inquiry Processes in the Social Sciences.* ERIC Document ED080413.

Mizell, H., and E. Gonzalez. 1991. *Disadvantaged Youth: Program Update.* New York: Edna McConnell Clark Foundation.

National Institute on Child Health and Development. 1992. *Annual Report, 1992.* Washington, DC: U.S. Department of Health, Education, and Welfare.

Nevin, Mary Lou. 1992. "A Language Arts Approach to Mathematics." *Arithmetic Teacher* 40(3): 142–46.

Oliner, P. M. 1986. "Legitimating and Implementing Prosocial Education." *Humboldt Journal of Social Relations* 13: 391–410.

Peters, Richard. 1985. *Cooperation. Our Common Home: Earth—A Curriculum Strategy to Affect Student Skills Development and Exposure to Diverse Global Natural/Social Environments.* ERIC Document ED267004.

Probst, Robert. 1986. "Mom, Wolfgang, and Me: Adolescent Literature, Critical Theory, and the English Classroom." *English Journal* 75(October): 33–39.

Ross, E. Wayne, and Lynne M. Hannay. 1987. "Reconsidering Reflective Inquiry: The Role of Critical Theory in the Teaching of Social Studies." *Southern Social Studies Quarterly* 13(2): 2–19.

Small, Robert. 1977. "The Junior Novel and the Art of Literature." *English Journal* 66(October): 56–59.

Smith, J. Lea, and Holly Johnson. 1993. "Bringing It Together: Literature in the Integrative Curriculum." *Middle School Journal* 25(1): 3–7.

Stevens, Alba. 1993. *Learning for Life Through Universal Themes: Literacy Improvement Series for Elementary Educators.* May. ERIC Document ED365851.

Stover, Lois, with Rita Karr. 1990. "Glastnost in the Classroom." *English Journal* 79: 47–53.

Syropoulos, M. 1990. *Efficacy: The Middle School Program Evaluation Report, 1989–1990.* Detroit, MI: Detroit Public Schools, Division of Management Effectiveness.

Tchudi, Stephen. 1991. *Travels Across the Curriculum.* New York: Scholastic.

1. vanAllen, Lanny. 1994. "English Language Arts Teachers Embracing Change and Making a Difference for Middle Grade Students." Paper presented at the National Council of Teachers of English Conference, Portland, Oregon, March 9.

2. Wiles, Jon, and Joseph Bondi. 1993. *The Essential Middle School*. New York: Macmillan.

# Young Adult Titles Cited

Adler, Carol S. 1986. *Kiss the Clown*. Boston: Hougton Mifflin.

Artenstein, Jeffrey. 1994. *Runaways*. New York: Tom Doherty.

Blacker, Terence. 1991. *Homebird*. London: Picadilly Press.

Brascum, Robbie. 1975. *Johnny May*. New York: Doubleday.

Bridgers, Sue Ellen. 1988. *Home Before Dark*. New York: Alfred Knopf.

Brooks, Bruce. 1986. *Midnight Hour Encores*. New York: HarperCollins.

Childress, Alice. 1973. *A Hero Ain't Nothin' but a Sandwich*. New York: Coward, McCann.

Cormier, Robert. 1974. *The Chocolate War*. New York: Pantheon.

Crutcher, Chris. 1986. *Stotan!* New York: Dell.

Danziger, Paula. 1974. *The Cat Ate My Gymsuit*. New York: Delacorte.

Dickinson, Peter. 1994. *Shadow of a Hero*. New York: Delacorte.

Filipovic, Zlata. 1994. *Zlata's Diary*. New York: Viking.

Fromm, Pete. 1994. *Monkey Tag*. New York: Scholastic.

George, Jean Craighead. 1995. *The Fire Bug Connection*. New York: Harper-Trophy.

Greene, Sheppard. 1988. *The Boy Who Drank Too Much*. New York: Dell Laurel-Leaf.

Hall, Lynn. 1987. *Flyaway*. New York: Charles Scribner's Sons.

Hawthorne, Nathaniel. 1887. "A Pine Tree Shilling." In *Stories of Our Country*, edited by James Johonnot. New York: D. Appleton.

Hiçyilmaz, Gaye. 1994. *Frozen Waterfall*. New York: Farrar, Strauss, Giroux.

Hinton, S. E. 1967. *The Outsiders*. New York: Viking.

———. 1971. *That Was Then, This Is Now*. New York: Viking.

Henegan, James. 1994. *Torn Away*. New York: Viking.

Johnson, Angela. 1993. *Toning the Sweep*. New York: Scholastic Hardcover.

Johnston, Norma. 1994. *The Image Game*. New York: Bridgewater Books.

Lasky, Kathryn. 1988. *The Bone Wars*. New York: William Morrow.

———. 1994. *Memoirs of a Bookbat*. New York: Harcourt Brace.

Likhanov, Albert. 1983. *Shadows Across the Sun*. New York: Harper and Row.

Lipsyte, Robert. 1987. *The Contender*. New York: Harper and Row.

Lyle, Katie Letcher. 1974. *Fair Day and Another Step Begun*. Philadelphia: J. P. Lippincott.

Lynch, Chris. 1994. *Gypsy Davey*. New York: HarperCollins.

Myers, Walter Dean. 1988. *Scorpions*. New York: HarperCollins.

———. 1994. *The Glory Field*. New York: Scholastic.

———. 1992. *Somewhere in the Darkness*. New York: Scholastic.

Naidoo, Beverly. 1990. *Chain of Fire*. Philadelphia: J. P. Lippincott.

Naylor, Phyllis. 1990. *Send No Blessings*. New York: Atheneum.

Oneal, Zibby. 1985. *In Summer Light*. New York: Viking/Kestral.

O'Brien, Robert. 1975. *Z for Zachariah*. New York: Atheneum.

Rodowsky, Colby. 1985. *Julie's Daughter*. New York: Farrar, Straus, Giroux.

Ruby, Lois. 1994. *Skin Deep*. New York: Scholastic Hardcover.

Rylant, Cynthia. 1989. *A Fine White Dust*. New York: Bradbury.

Samuels, Gertrude. 1989. *Yours, Brett*. New York: New American Library.

Spinelli, Jerry. 1985. *Space Station Seventh Grade*. New York: Dell.

———. 1985. *Night of the Whale*. Boston: Little, Brown.

Taylor, Mildred. 1976. *Roll of Thunder, Hear My Cry*. New York: Dial.

Vail, Rachel. 1994. *Ever After*. New York: Orchard (Richard Jackson).

Voigt, Cynthia. 1992. *Orfe*. New York: Scholastic.

Wolff, Virginia Euwer. 1993. *Make Lemonade*. New York: Scholastic.

Zindel, Paul. 1969. *The Pigman*. New York: HarperCollins.

# Two

# There's No Place Like Home

At the end of *The Wizard of Oz* Dorothy chants, "There's no place like home, there's no place like home" while clicking the heels of her ruby slippers together. Having realized that what she wanted was in her own backyard, having come to recognize the importance of her family and her home for her happiness, Dorothy finally is able to use the magic of the slippers to transport herself back to Auntie Em and life on the farm in Kansas.

In many ways, Dorothy represents a fairly typical tension felt by many adolescents—she is eager to have an adventure, she delights in making new friends and in working with them for a common goal, but she understands that home provides a sense of security and safety that she does not have in Oz. Since middle level students are beginning to experience that desire to establish their identities outside the family, a unit titled "There's No Place Like Home" can provide a structure for exploring what "home" can and should mean, for thinking about the varieties of "home" that exist, and for beginning to consider the kind of home they may want to create for themselves in the future.

## Rationale

Having a home of one's own is a desire that crosses cultural boundaries, a value that has been expressed throughout history and in all corners of the world. In today's society, when homelessness is common, when poverty and war have created generations of children who know only refugee camps as home, and when so many children experience only abuse and neglect at home, there is still the desire on the part of young people to find a place where they can be themselves. A sixth-grade teacher at Southeast Middle School in Baltimore City, finds that her unit "There's No Place Like Home" provides the structure her students need to discuss significant issues related to the concept of "home." Her students come from diverse backgrounds representing varied cultural and ethnic groups. They reflect the diversity of home and family that exist in today's society—some live in shelters, some have traditional two-parent homes, some live with foster parents, some live with grandparents, and some live with one parent. Some of her students come from several generations of welfare recipients; others come from fairly well-to-do families. All of them, however, as middle school students, are beginning to be concerned with how their home shapes their sense of who they are, and how they will go about creating homes of their own in the future.

Consider the following statistics that demonstrate the difficulties inherent in defining "home" in today's society.

1. Hodgkinson (1991) reports that as of 1988, 4.3 million children were living with a mother who had never married, that almost 50 percent of America's children will spend some time before age eighteen being raised by a single parent, and that almost 4 million school-age children are being raised by neither parent.

2. Edwards and Young (1992) find that at any given time, 25 percent of all American children live with just one parent.

3. Kaywell (1993) citing the Child Abuse Council, notes that in the United States there are over 2 million cases of child abuse each year; almost 25 percent of all children will be sexually abused before they reach adulthood (92).

4. Gil (1990) finds that in 78 percent of abuse cases, the abuse has been performed by a member of the victim's immediate family.

5. Hodgkinson (1991) also states that at least one-fourth of all preschool children live in poverty, and that 40 percent of all uses of shelters for the homeless are for families with children.

6. Linehan (1992) reports that on any given night, between 68,000 to 500,000 children are homeless.

Many students take "home" for granted. Home is a place of warmth, shelter, nourishment, security, and love, a place where they are accepted and respected regardless of their performance in the world outside the home. But clearly, "home" is not such an idyllic place for all students. For some, there is no home to which to go after school, so school becomes that safe haven, that place of warmth and shelter. For others, "home" does not equate with security; instead it is a place where emotional, physical, and sexual abuse occurs. It is not a place where they feel nurtured and respected and cared for. Whether or not young adults have a home, they are beginning to think about what a home can and should be, and about the kind of home they want when they get older.

## Unit Goals

Individual teachers working within the specific contexts of their schools and curricula will want to add to and subtract from the following list of goals for this unit. Also, teachers working with students engaged in inquiry will find that different groups of students will pose different questions; thus, the unit goals may be framed in different ways for various classes. In general, students will develop speaking, listening, reading, and writing skills, as well as critical and creative thinking skills. More specifically, the unit will allow students to be able to:

1. Read a title from those provided of their own choosing and discuss its relationship to a unit on "home."
2. Describe the relationship between the setting of the story and the concept of "home."
3. Define "home" using personal experiences, literary examples, and information from science and social studies lessons.
4. Describe strategies used in creating a home.
5. Predict plot events based on understanding of the characters, settings, and conflicts involved in the literature.
6. Compare and contrast literary works sharing the theme of "home."
7. Research the concept of "home" from a variety of perspectives, including library research on scientific definitions, interviews with people of various age groups, and primary source material and historical fiction about "homes" in different time periods.
8. Synthesize the unit content in a personally meaningful way through a group presentation or performance.

## Annotations of the Text Set

The sixth graders at Southeast Middle School read one of the titles below marked with an asterisk; the other titles could just as easily be incorporated into a transdisciplinary unit designed to engage middle grade students in a study of how "home" can be defined and how one's home affects one's sense of self.

**Bennett, James. 1994. *Dakota Dream*. New York: Scholastic.**

After years in foster homes, fifteen-year-old Floyd decides to search for a home on his own. He ends up on a Sioux reservation, and after experiencing a "vision quest," learns more about what it means to be a member of the Sioux family. As a result, he finds a sense of place and community.

**Blacker, Terence. 1991. *Homebird*. London: Pan Piper (Pan Macmillan Children's Books).**

Nicky Morrison thought he had a fairly typical kind of life, until he feels compelled to run away from the world war that has erupted in his family, and finds himself living on the run and getting involved with the law.

**Bode, Janet, and Stan Mack. 1994. *Heartbreak and Roses: Real Life Stories of Troubled Love*. New York: Delacorte.**

Both group discussions and one-on-one interviews with teenagers provided Bode and Mack with the insights they share in this book about the ways in which young people search for a center, a sense of identity, and a sense of acceptance through their relationships.

**Choi, Sook Nyul. 1994. *Gathering of Pearls*. Boston: Houghton Mifflin.**

Sookan Bak, whom readers may have met previously in *The Year of Impossible Goodbyes* and *Echoes of the White Giraffe*, has left her family behind in Korea. She is now on her own attending college in the United States, but she still feels torn between the expectations of her family and her own dreams for a different kind of future.

**Christopher, John. 1994. *A Dusk of Demons*. New York: Macmillan.**

This fantasy tale tells of Ben's horrifying adventure in quest for family and home as he deals with demons, the Dark One, and the people whom they have intimidated into depression and distrust of strangers.

**Cleary, Beverly. 1983. *Dear Mr. Henshaw*. New York: Dell.**

Leigh Botts, a sixth grader, is upset by his parents' divorce. He writes letters to his favorite author, Mr. Henshaw, in an effort to come to terms with the changes in his life. Eventually, the letters become diary entries as Leigh learns the value of writing to express his feelings and his perceptions of his father and his new family situation.

**Fox, Paula. 1991. *Monkey Island*. New York: Orchard Books.**

Clay Garrity lives on the streets of New York after first his father, and then his mother, abandon him. At age eleven, it is difficult for Clay to reconcile his new situation with his memories of the comfortable home he knew before his father lost his job. He is determined to wait for his mother and to stay away from the authorities. Befriended by Calvin and Buddy, who live in a crate in the park, Clay discovers a new sense of family and home, and he develops a new perspective on the shadows that "are other people trying to sleep on stone" (79).

**Henegan, James. 1994. *Torn Away*. New York: Viking (Penguin).**

Declan, a thirteen-year-old terrorist from Northern Ireland, has been caught and sent to Canada to live with his Uncle Matthew and family, all pacifists. He must choose between a home on the streets of Belfast surrounded by other young terrorists and a home in the wilds of Canada surrounded by people who come to care about him, and about whom he comes to care as well.

**Holman, Felice. 1983. *The Wild Children*. New York: Charles Scribner's Sons.**

Alex, a twelve-year-old boy left behind when his family is taken away by the secret police in the aftermath of the Bolshevik Revolution, tells how he joins with other homeless children—the "bezprizorni" researched by the author—to create a new kind of family and to survive through their collaborative efforts.

**Lasky, Katherine. 1994. *Memoirs of a Bookbat*. New York: Harcourt Brace and Company.**

When Harper's parents become "migrants for God" and begin to impose their values on her, this fourteen-year-old must determine whether or not she can live in the home they provide and still retain her sense of self.

**MacLachlan, Patricia. 1991. *Journey*. New York: Doubleday.**

When he is eleven, Journey's mother leaves him and his sister with their grandparents, shredding pictures from their family album before she goes. Journey tries to put the pieces back together, and also searches through the pictures his grandfather takes in an effort to provide Journey with a past. In the process, Journey finds some clues about why his mother left and about the love that still exists to bind his family together.

**Maguire, Gregory. 1994. *Missing Sisters*. New York: Margaret K. McElderry Books.**

Alice, physically handicapped and living in an orphanage, searches for clues to her past and to her identity, learning in the process to value the home she already does have and learning to recognize the importance of the family she has always had.

**Myers, Christopher A., and Lynne Borne. 1994.** *Forest of the Clouded Leopard.* **Boston: Houghton Mifflin.**

Kenchendai, fifteen, has to rescue his father from the land of the dead, a quest that takes him into the jungles of Borneo. He has to confront himself and begin to make peace between the world of science and technology in which he lives while at school, and the world of Iban mythology and spirits where he finds his "private heart."

**Myers, Walter Dean. 1992.** *Somewhere in the Darkness.* **New York: Scholastic.**

Jimmy Little arrives home from school one day to be greeted by a tall, thin man who introduces himself as Jimmy's father. Jimmy then embarks on a mission to clear his father's name, but the father-son trip from New York to Chicago and Arkansas results in more unanswered questions about Creb Little's convict past.

**Paterson, Katherine. 1978.** *The Great Gilly Hopkins.* **New York: Harper and Row.**

Gilly has been bumped from foster home to foster home, and she's become adept at asserting herself, at gaining control of wherever she's placed. Then, she meets Maime Trotter and begins to experience a different sense of home and family than she's had before.

**Pfeffer, Susan Beth. 1994.** *Twice Taken.* **New York: Delacorte.**

Brooke, born Amy, learns that her father abducted her when she was quite young. Now, she has to live with her mother and her mother's family, and everyone has to learn the difference between liking and loving as they all adjust to having Amy "home"—especially since she is not certain that she has, in fact, come home.

**Roybal, Laura. 1994.** *Billy.* **Boston: Houghton Mifflin.**

All of a sudden the life sixteen-year-old Billy has been leading comes crashing down around him when Dave, his stepfather and legal guardian, arrives in New Mexico to take him back to Iowa and the family he has not seen during the years he has been living with his natural father. He feels like he is living the kidnapping all over again, and he struggles to figure out who he is, what it means to be part of the family, and how to define and fit into a new home.

**Rylant, Cynthia. 1993.** *Missing May.* **New York: Dell.**

For years after her mother's death, Summer was passed from relative to relative. Finally, when she was six, Uncle Ob and Aunt May took her into their home, a trailer in West Virginia. Now, at twelve, Summer narrates the quest for new sense of family she and Uncle Ob undertake in the wake of the death of their beloved May.

**Rylant, Cynthia. *Something Permanent*. Photographs by Walker Evans. 1993. San Diego: Harcourt Brace Children's Books.**

During the 1930s, Walker Evans wandered the United States attempting to document "America" through photographs commissioned by the Farm Security Administration. His black-and-white photos tell the stories of individuals striving to create lives and homes for themselves while surviving the extreme conditions of the Great Depression. Cynthia Rylant has now given voice to the people captured through Walker's art. Together, the poems and the photos combine to create a reverent and compelling vision of lives lived in another time and place.

**Thesman, Jean. 1994. *Cattail Moon*. Boston: Houghton Mifflin.**

Julie finds herself torn between her mother's home in the city and her father's home in rural Moon Valley. While working out the solutions to a mystery-shrouded romance from the past, she learns that she has to stand up for herself and her dreams in order to feel at home in any setting.

Additionally, there are a number of titles annotated in Appendix B that would also work well in "There's No Place Like Home." Creative teachers and students could add to this unit by reviewing those annotations and by finding works on their own as well to supplement it. The titles here do, however, reflect attention to cultural diversity—*Somewhere in the Darkness*, *Gathering of Pearls*, and *Dakota Dream*, among others, have protagonists from varied cultural backgrounds. *Forest of the Clouded Leopard*, with its setting in the rain forest of Borneo, and *The Wild Children*, with its setting in post–Bolshevik Revolution Russia, provide rich sources of material to mine for science and social studies content. There are titles here that might appeal to both male and female readers: *Cattail Moon* is about a young woman; *Torn Away* is about a young man. Some titles, such as *The Great Gilly Hopkins*, are easier to read than others, such as *Dakota Dream*, which require more sophisticated reading skill. Also, a variety of genres is reflected in this list: nonfiction, poetry, fantasy, and realistic novels. The point is that in creating a list of titles useful for transdisciplinary study, issues of cultural diversity, of gender appeal, and of reading ability and special needs all must be considered.

## Unit Activities

Initially, to activate students' cognitive structures and tap their background of experience, a strategy such as "pyramiding" is useful. Students individually attempt to define "home" in one sentence. Then they work with a partner to create a combined definition. Two sets of partners, now a group of four, write a definition that encompasses the thoughts of each group member. The groups of four can then be combined into larger groups of eight, and so on, until, eventually, the class reaches consensus on a definition. This definition becomes a touchstone for their reading; as students read their texts and study the concept of home from other perspectives, they can add to and change this definition.

Other possible introductory activities might include role playing situations about home; watching portions of a video such as *Medicine Man* (1991)—about a tribe of people in the Brazilian rain forest and how the encroachment of logging roads into their environment affects their sense of home; reading poetry about home, such as Robert Frost's "Death of a Hired Hand" (1939) that includes the line "Home is the place that, when you go there, / they have to take you in"; or listening to a member of the local community talk about how that community has changed over time, and how those changes have affected the individual's sense of home. Students might watch bits of videotaped news broadcasts about the plight of the homeless in their community and then engage in a *k/w/l* activity, brainstorming what they *know* about the situation, and what they *want* to learn and then, at the end of the unit, making a list of what they have *learned*. They might take a field trip to a nature center and learn more about the natural habitats of indigenous wildlife and how changes in the local environment are affecting the homes of local wild creatures. If there are recent immigrants from other countries in the school, and if these students would feel comfortable answering questions about their experiences in moving from one home to another, asking them to share their perceptions on home also works well as a bridge into the unit.

After the initiating activity, Rebecca Joseph, the teacher from Southeast Middle School introduces the core texts for the unit by book talking the various titles from which students then choose a book for independent reading. These book talks include the kind of information *her students* have indicated they value knowing about a title when trying to determine whether or not it might be of interest to them. They have told her that when they are choosing a title, they want to know about print size, number of pages, whether or not a text was illustrated, something about the author, and the kinds of characters involved. Joseph's book talks, therefore, include this information as well as a personal "bridge"—a story of how the book had affected the teacher as reader; a quote from the text—an oral reading illustrating something of the author's style and of the important literary aspects of the text; a plot overview; and a brief statement assessing the merits of the book. Students then make lists of their top three choices; of the titles Joseph used, *Somewhere in the Darkness*, because of its African American characters, and *Dear Mr. Henshaw* and *The Great Gilly Hopkins* because of their humorous tone and big print, usually are the most popular.

Joseph then gives each student one of the titles they have requested, and, for the first week of the unit, she provides time in class for the students to read their selection; usually she devotes at least half of her fifty-minute period to reading. Each day, they complete a journal assignment as a drill about their book. These journal topics are designed to ensure students are understanding their reading on a literal level. For instance, one day they may be told to "Describe the setting. Where does this book take place?" Another day, they might be instructed to "Describe the major characters and where they are living. Why are they living where they are?" As they read more of the book, they have questions to answer that allow them to think more globally about the title, such as "Why do you think your book is in this unit?" or "Describe any other books or movies that you have seen which might fit into this unit."

Once the students have had the opportunity to read significant portions of the text, they begin to work in small groups to collaborate and construct a sense of the text in a communal way. In preparation for small-group discussions, the drill/warm-up journal activities also include topics such as "How did you feel about yesterday's conversation with your group? What did you learn from it?"

Joseph, as an English language arts teacher acting in isolation and not as part of a transdisciplinary team, emphasizes literary content and related skills as the unit unfolds. Initially, students work with others who have read the same titles. She prompts these discussions with sentence starters such as "I feel strongly about . . ."; "I agree/disagree with . . ."; "I don't understand . . ."; and "I predict. . . ." After discussions based on these prompts, students engage in "marathon writes" about the group process, describing how the discussion flowed, how individual group members contributed, what questions arose from the discussion, and what strategies the group might use in the future in order to ensure that everyone participate equally. Her goals for these discussions are to ensure that everyone knows the basics of the plot, understands character relationships and functions within the story, and can describe the ways in which the setting influenced both character actions and plot tensions.

As a culminating activity, Joseph asks students who have read the same titles to generate a "performance" based on their reading that will show their peers who have not read that title how the main character found a place called home. They brainstorm possibilities, such as video ads for the book, bulletin boards, or "big books" as a class before the groups begin their task. Students receive collective grades for their performances, and they are held individually account-able for the information presented in all the performances, as well as for completion of the drill questions and for participation in the small-group discussions.

After learning about all the titles, students work individually to define "home" in a personal way, by completing the sentence, "I think home is a place where . . ." Students talk about home as a place "where I am safe," "where someone loves me," or, on a very rudi-mentary level, as "a place where I can sleep." Generalizing about the meaning of "home" across cultural boundaries and across individual experiences, drawing on their vicarious experience as readers of vari-ous titles, the students begin to define home in more complex ways— as being a place where the individual is taken care of, takes care of others, and shares his or her problems. They begin to recognize, as Gilly from *The Great Gilly Hopkins* did, that "home" is within the indi-vidual; each person has to accept responsibility for generating his or her own home and sense of the future.

## Transdisciplinary Connections

For the unit described here to become more clearly transdisciplinary in nature, students would have to explore the concept of "home" more explicitly from the point of view of the scientist, historian, or artist. But the seeds of such investigation are evident already in this unit as pre-sented. Although *the teacher* currently brings the unit to a close in a formal manner with the student presentations, this might be the time when more genuine inquiry, meaning the posing of questions by *the students* based on the very rich and complex knowledge base they now have about "home," might begin. Building on their knowledge of the literary texts, students can easily begin to examine issues embedded in them from other perspectives. For instance, Gilly Hopkins is a foster child; Leigh Botts is the child of divorce; Maniac McGee lives on the streets for a time. Students can easily be led into investigations of statistics about homelessness in their community, or about the pros and cons of foster care, and can engage in projects such as writing editorials that demonstrate their point of view on these issues.

Given the diversity of cultural contexts in which the main char-acters strive to create a place called home, and given the fact that titles such as *Something Permanent*, with its black-and-white photos of the South during the Depression, or *Forest of the Clouded Leopard*, set in Borneo, provide insight into the realities and issues involved in creating "home" in diverse situations, there are several ways that other content area teachers on the team, planning together, could have extended the study of "home" through their disciplines. Marcincin, in a 1992 article, describes a transdisciplinary unit on homelessness that incorporates art, home economics, English, math, and social studies activities.

In Chapter 1, there is a list of the kinds of questions that teachers and students should generate as a way to focus their study during a particular unit. Here are examples of such questions for "There's No Place Like Home":

1. Sample unit question: What is a "home" and who is responsible for creating "home"?

2. Sample focusing questions for generating discipline-based problems: What are the requisite components of "home"? What strategies are useful in creating "home"?

3. What are some sample disciplinary problems related to question #2?

> *Math:* What are the uses and values of the "home" key on the computer? Task: Design a computer program to understand and manipulate the concept of "home base."

> *Science:* How does the environment affect home and habitat for both groups of people and various animals? Task: Through library and newspaper research as well as through use of computer-based technologies, examine how current environmental problems, such as acid rain, the greenhouse effect, and other kinds of pollution, have affected efforts to create "home," and describe adaptive techniques used by various groups in response to these changes in the environment.

> *Social studies:* How have cultural, economic, and technological changes affected human efforts to create homes in various climates, countries, and social conditions? Task: Explore the issue of homelessness and write a letter to an influential member of the community outlining your ideas for helping to ameliorate the situation based on research within your community. Buller (1980) describes how the work of several Native American authors, including Momaday and Silko, can be used to show students the different sense of place, ritual, and community that exists among various Native American peoples.

> *Language arts:* What does "home" mean to different individuals? Task: Create a personal definition of the ideal home and outline at least five factors that will affect your individual efforts to achieve this ideal.

*Health:* How does home life contribute either positively or negatively to the development of personal identity and to stress? Task: Create a scrapbook or portfolio that shows the contributions of your home to your identity.

*Physical education:* Is "home" a concept that appears in games and sports from various cultures? Task: Generalize about the meaning of "home" as it applies to various game situations.

*Art:* How do individual artists deal with the concept of home in their body of work? Task: Create a visual representation of the personal ideal of home generated in language arts.

*Music:* How might "home" be said to relate to music theory (major/minor/diminished/augmented chords, for instance)? Task: Choose music to reflect the personal ideal of home generated in language arts.

In an inquiry-based classroom, the teacher's job is to facilitate the building of a knowledge base sufficient for students to be motivated to pose questions (Harste and Short 1995). The questions provided here certainly can lead to interesting and exciting lessons, and a team of teachers, each well-versed in a different discipline, could plan interrelated class sessions based on them. How much more enthusiastic students would be, however, if *they* were given some ownership of the curriculum by being taught to ask their own questions.

When Dorothy utters the well-known phrase "There's no place like home," it is clear that she has learned an important lesson. For Dorothy, life with her uncle and Auntie Em on their Kansas farm provides everything she needs; as Glinda tells her, everything she has been looking for, she can find right there. Not all young people are as lucky. The address some give when filling out school and other state agency forms may not be a "home"; they may not even have an address to note. They need some place where they can feel a sense of home and belonging. As Harper writes, in *Memoirs of a Bookbat*:

As I lay in bed that night, I thought about that alluring word [belong]. To belong did not mean ownership. You were not someone's property. The "be" syllable was about existence: "to be" yourself and "to be" in a special place that no one else could occupy within your family except you. The "long" part was about the heart, a place in the heart where a family met and lived together. They just didn't put up with each other. They longed for each other. To belong was not a state of mind but a state of heart. (161)

# Works Cited

Buller, Galen. 1980. "New Interpretations of Native American Literature: A Survival Technique." *American Indian Culture and Research Journal* 4(1–2): 165–77.

Edwards, P. A., and L. S. J. Young. 1992. "Beyond Parents: Family, School and Community Involvement." *Phi Delta Kappan* 74(1): 72–80.

Frost, Robert. 1939. "Death of a Hired Hand." In *The Complete Poems of Robert Frost.* New York: Henry Holt.

Gil, Eliana. 1990. *Treatment of Adult Survivors of Child Abuse.* 2d ed. Oakland, CA: Launch Press.

Harste, Jerome, and Kathy Short. 1995. "Inquiry, Theme Cycles, and Interdisciplinary Teaching." Presentation made at the National Council of Teachers of English Spring Conference, Minneapolis, March.

Hodgkinson, H. 1991. "Reform Versus Reality." *Phi Delta Kappan* 73(1): 8–16.

Kaywell, Joan. 1993. *Adolescents at Risk.* Westport, CT: Greenwood Press.

Lasky, Kathryn. 1994. *Memoirs of a Bookbat.* New York: Harcourt Brace.

Linehan, M. F. 1992. "Children Who Are Homeless: Educational Strategies for School Personnel." *Phi Delta Kappan* 74(1): 61–66.

Marcincin, Linda. 1992. "Getting Involved: An Interdisciplinary Project on Homelessness." *Schools in the Middle* 1(3): 6–10.

*Medicine Man.* 1991. Buena Vista/Touchstone Pictures. 106 minutes. Videocassette.

# Three

# Conflict and Confrontation

During the spring of 1995, I surveyed 339 very diverse middle school students, asking them to rate their interest in all of the transdisciplinary thematic concepts listed in Appendix B. Some students came from suburban, fairly affluent schools with high numbers of professional parents; others came from neighborhoods in which families exist on limited incomes and in which factories and heavy industry, such as Bethlehem Steel, are the primary employers. Other students attend an inner city school with a population that is 97 percent African American and that is diverse in terms of economic status. Still others take part in a magnet school program geared toward science and technology at an inner-city school with a mix of students from diverse ethnic backgrounds.

Both males and females from all the responding schools rated their interest in a unit on "conflict" very highly; it received a mean score of 4.6941 on a scale of 1 to 5, with 5 as the highest level of potential interest. The concept receiving the next highest mean score was "survival," at 3.982; clearly "conflict" is much more on the minds and in the hearts of the middle schools students surveyed than any of the other concepts presented to them. (The survey instrument and the results of the statistical analysis are provided in Appendix A.)

One young woman, in an unsolicited written comment, noted her interest in this topic was very high because she sees evidence of conflict in a variety of aspects of everyday life. She writes, "There are many arguments about color and looks, and it is important to understan[d] everyone. There are many obosed [abused] and melested [molested] children and they need to learn how to deal with conflict. It is important to show that people have many different cultures and should not have conflict because of them." It seems to me that this writer expresses the middle school student's growing concern for understanding the world in which he or she lives and indicates the awareness that conflict is a part of that world, both on an individual level, as he or she attempts to find a personal identity, and on a societal level, as groups of individuals attempt to sort out their differences in a world that grows increasingly smaller and more crowded.

# Rationale

Conflict is an integral part of daily life, and a concern that, like the concern for finding a home of one's own, crosses cultural, gender, and age boundaries. Dealing with conflict is a survival skill that middle school students are beginning to be able to learn, given their growing facility for formal operational thinking and their decreasing egocentrism. At the same time, middle school students seem to live in a constant state of conflict. Their emotions pull them internally in a thousand directions at once. They squabble with their peers, they argue with their parents, they rebel against the authority of their teachers, and they view with dismay the proof that adults cannot seem to find ways for the countries of the world to live in peace. As they engage in the process of defining a self, of creating an individual identity, they must deal with internal conflicts about their values, morals, and ethics. They are capable of examining the ways in which characters resolve conflicts and of exploring alternative responses to conflict situations which may result in quite different consequences for all concerned.

# Unit Goals

Individual teachers working within the specific contexts of their own classrooms and within given curricular constraints will be able to adapt the following list of goals to suit their specific situations. In general, throughout the unit, students will develop their social skills and all their language processing skills—listening, speaking, reading, and writing—as well as their ability to solve problems and to think critically and creatively. More specifically, the unit will allow students to:

1. Engage in collaborative response to and analysis of a literary work read by the entire class focused on the theme of "conflict"; examine the conflicting nature of male and female responses to that work.

2. Compare and contrast individually read titles to the in-common text based on the author's treatment of and perspective on "conflict." Define and apply the literary concepts of "individual against individual," "individual against self," "individual against

society," and "individual against nature" as they relate to the author's craft in creating plot tensions and interest on the part of the reader.

3. Define "conflict" and ways to deal with it creatively and productively, drawing on personal experiences, literary examples, and lessons developed to show how the concept can be explored from the perspectives of professionals in all the traditional content areas.

4. Describe how "conflict" is important in a literary work, defining the relationship between conflict and plot, and character interactions.

5. Collect information from a variety of sources about the nature of "conflict," and determine a set of personal goals related to solving a specific conflict on an individual basis.

6. Participate in an outdoor education experience designed to develop team spirit and to help enhance conflict resolution skills; hypothesize about the ways in which the setting in which conflict occurs affects the conflict resolution process.

7. Investigate historically how nations and cultures have dealt with conflicts related to differing values, differing perceptions of borderlines, and differing worldviews.

8. Research the nature of conflict in the natural world.

9. Generate questions related to the concept and its significance in daily life and develop procedures and a resource list useful in answering these questions.

10. Synthesize the unit content by creating a product for a public exhibition on "Conflict and Confrontation."

## Annotations of the Text Set

For this unit, any one of the following titles could be selected, based on availability, potential student interest, reading ability, and other criteria for in-common reading. Thus, in this unit, students will share the experience of reading the same title, and consideration of conflict as it appears in that text will form the basis for daily lessons. Additionally, students can be asked to read at least one, or possibly two, more titles on their own. Then, they can bring to bear the perspective of these texts on the large-group discussions centered on the in-common reading, or they can work in small groups to extend their understanding of conflict in a variety of ways.

**Choi, Sook Nyul. 1993.** *Echoes of the White Giraffe.* **Boston: Houghton Mifflin.**

In this sequel to *The Year of Impossible Goodbyes,* Sookan, now fifteen, adjusts to life in the refugee village of Pusan, but she longs for the end to the civil war raging in Korea and for the chance for her family to reunite in Seoul.

**Hinojosa, Maria. 1995.** *Crews: Gang Members Talk to Maria Hinojosa.* **New York: Harcourt Brace.**

*Crews* is a sampling of NPR reporter Hinojosa's interviews with young men and women who live lives of violence on the edge of poverty in our urban areas.

**Hunt, Irene. 1964.** *Across Five Aprils.* **New York: Follet.**

A young man learns just how devastating war can be when his brothers choose to fight on opposite sides in the American Civil War.

**Lee, Harper. 1960.** *To Kill a Mockingbird.* **Philadelphia: Lippincott.**

Scout, a young girl, tells the story of life in a small southern town, and of her father's decision, in the face of that town's sense of values and propriety, to defend a Black man whom he believes innocent of the crime of which he is accused.

**Lee, Marie. 1994.** *Saying Goodbye.* **Boston: Houghton Mifflin.**

When Korean American Ellen Sung goes to Harvard and meets her African American roommate, she has to confront her biases. She finds herself taking unexpected stands and testing the limits of friendship.

**Miklowitz, Gloria D. 1985.** *The War Between the Classes.* **New York: Delacorte.**

Amy and Adam are in love, but their feelings for each other are being tested not only by their parents, whose social class and cultural differences make accepting Amy and Adam's relationship difficult, but also by their involvement at their high school in "The Color Game," designed to make students aware of their various prejudices.

**Naidoo, Beverly. 1990.** *Chain of Fire.* **Philadelphia: Lippincott.**

When her South African village is moved to a "homeland," her school closed, and the water supply shut off, fifteen-year-old Naledi and her friends find themselves demonstrating against these specific actions and against apartheid in general.

**Namioka, Lensey. 1994.** *April and the Dragon Lady.* **New York: Browndeer Press (Harcourt Brace).**

High school student April Chen, feeling herself to be "a minority of one," fights for her independence from the traditions of her manipulative grandmother's world, while struggling to retain a sense of self as she enters her first serious relationship.

**Patent, Dorothy Hinshaw. 1994.** *The Vanishing Feast: How Dwindling Genetic Diversity Threatens the World's Food Supply.* **New York: Gulliver Green (Harcourt Brace).**

What is "biodiversity"? Why should we be concerned about the loss of diversity among plants and animals? What historical lessons must we learn about the importance of protecting ourselves from disaster associated with diminishing biodiversity? Are we too late to do anything about this issue? These and other questions are explored by Patent, who holds a doctorate in zoology, as she describes what biodiversity is and how we can preserve it.

**Strasser, Todd. 1985.** *A Very Touchy Subject.* **New York: Delacorte.**

Should Scott confront Paula with his knowledge of the young man who's been crawling out of her window at the same time each morning?

**Tate, Eleanora. 1987.** *The Secret of Gumbo Grove.* **Franklin-Watts.**

Raisin is talked into cleaning up the old church cemetery. In the process she digs up a mystery nobody in town wants to talk about, leaving her to decide whether the past should be exposed or whether it is better left buried.

**Westall, Robert. 1992.** *Gulf.* **London: Metheun Children's Books.**

Tom tells how his younger brother, Figgis, "becomes" an Arab soldier named Latif who perishes in the Gulf War.

**Wolff, Virginia Euwer. 1994.** *Make Lemonade.* **New York: Scholastic.**

LaVaughn is fourteen and she needs a job; Jolly is seventeen, the mother of two children, and she needs help. In poetic stream-of-consciousness prose, LaVaughn tells what happens when the two of them join forces, learning about caring, responsibility, and trust in the midst of a culture of poverty.

Of course, given the central role of conflict in plot development, almost any novel could be used as the basis for this unit. Teachers and students can use their imaginations to combine titles listed in Appendix

B under different headings in unique ways when developing a unit on "Conflict," and can select titles they discover on their own as well.

Several teachers (Huhtala 1994; Bettendorf 1987) have described interdisciplinary units centered around the concept of "War" in articles in which they share both the content and approaches they have used. Kennemer (1994) provides a very detailed bibliography, divided into sections based on various wars, including the Revolutionary War, Vietnam, and both World Wars. For the purposes of this chapter, *Gulf* by Robert Westall (1992) will be used to introduce the broader concepts of conflict and confrontation.

In *Gulf*, Tom and Andy are fairly ordinary adolescent brothers, though Tom has known right from birth that Andy, nicknamed Figgis, needs "a lot of looking after" (11). What is really unusual about Figgis is that he has "things" for people and animals. "Obsessions." When he was only six, he became captivated by a photo in the *Guardian* of a witch doctor. He *knew* all about the man, even *knew* his name. The family began to recognize Figgis' strangeness when they managed to learn that the man's name really was what Figgis had said it was. Then, the Gulf War begins. First Figgis begins talking in a strange foreign tongue. His face takes on different proportions. He begins scratching himself all over. Eventually Tom determines that Figgis, always sensitive to the pain of others, has been "taken over" by Latif, a boy from the Gulf, whose perceptions of the war are quite different than those Tom and his family receive from the newspaper.

Gulf is short, only ninety-three pages, but it packs quite an emotional wallop because of the different view of "reality" of the Gulf War that the reader is given from Latif's point of view. It provides insights into the nature of conflicts between nations and into the conflicted nature of the self. Family conflict, conflicting medical opinions, and internal conflict all are significant elements of this novel. Therefore, it prompts lots of questions: What was the Persian Gulf conflict really about? Were there options other than the one chosen by the U.S. for dealing with the crisis? How is knowledge constructed? Whose knowledge should weigh the most heavily in decision making? What are the limits of medical science's knowledge about the human brain, and what should doctors do who confront those limitations? How do family dynamics change when a member is torn apart inside? And, how does Westall, as artist, use conflict to advance his plot, develop his theme, and evoke a response in his readers?

## Unit Activities

Because middle level students are constantly involved in conflicts and confrontations, beginning the unit by simply webbing "conflict" allows them to tap those experiences by brainstorming specific examples of conflict in their lives. Prior to the first class, the teacher puts huge pieces of chart paper on the wall to make a large writing surface and gives each student entering the room a magic marker, telling them to contribute to the web. (Sometimes I make the web unstructured, starting merely with "conflict" ringed in the middle of the page. Other times, I structure the web, putting spokes off of the central term with labels such as "synonyms," "antonyms," "examples of conflict—personal," "examples of conflict—in the world," "reasons for," "ways to prevent," and so on. Either way, allowing students to be physically active and to engage in the collaborative production of the web makes sense given the developmental stage of middle level learners.)

What often will happen, in a class of at least average size, is that some small "conflicts" will erupt as students attempt to complete the activity. As they bump elbows, "steal" each other's ideas, or crowd around the writing surface, evidence of conflict may emerge. The teacher then uses these examples and the content of the web the students generate to guide the students through a categorization exercise, asking them to group the examples into categories that make sense to them in some way. The traditional literary categories of conflict will emerge from this discussion: individual against individual, individual against self, individual against society, and individual against nature, though other categorization schemes may emerge.

Another activity I have used to generate the same categories of conflict and to probe students' prior knowledge of and experience with the term "conflict" is one advocated by Cowen and Cowen (1980) in *Writing* called "Cubing." The point of the exercise is to help the writer explore a topic from six different perspectives (the "sides of the cube") in quick succession, gathering a great deal of insight and information out of which a thesis and more formal writing then can grow:

1. Describe "conflict"—try to write a dictionary definition, describing the term in a fairly matter-of-fact way.

2. Compare and contrast the concept of "conflict" to other concepts or make analogies and metaphors—perhaps compare it to "confrontation" or "war." It is OK to make a string of comparisons or to elaborate on one that strikes your fancy.

3. Associate the term with personal experience—describe incidents from your life that seemed key factors in determining your concept of "conflict" or write any other kind of personal reflection on the term.

4. Analyze "conflict"—try to be objective, almost scientific, in describing the constituent parts of the concept.

5. Apply "conflict"—describe what conflict is good for, how it is useful/necessary in everyday life.

6. Argue for or against the notion of "conflict" as an inherent part of existence—take a stand. It is OK to be silly, serious, or anything in between.

After completing the freewriting, students work in groups to share the insights they have generated through exploring the topic from the diverse perspectives, attempting to categorize the kinds of conflict about which they wrote; or, in a large-group discussion, the teacher can guide the students to create such categories.

After processing either the webbing activity or the "cubing," the teacher asks the students to use all of the information at their disposal to generate a hypothesis of some sort about the nature of "conflict" and its significance in their lives. Each group of students is likely to generate a different hypothesis because each group of individuals will have a different set of experiences upon which to draw for so doing. It is important that the teacher *not* impose a hypothesis on the group.

For example, in developing their hypothesis, students may focus on the reasons for conflict. They may talk about destructiveness of unresolved conflict in daily life, or they may even come up with a rather surprising perspective, as one group of students did when they agreed on the hypothesis, "Conflict is an inevitable and potentially useful part of life."

Once the students have generated a hypothesis, the next step is defining terms. Whatever the hypothesis is, the teacher has to guide the students to a consensus on definitions. Using the sample hypothesis from the previous paragraph, students would have to define, for the purposes of their inquiries, the following terms: conflict, inevitable, potentially, and useful. At this point, the teacher introduces the book for in-common reading and book-talks the choices available for independent work, generalizing about them in the process. The Choi title is autobiographical and recounts historical events; although fiction, the Naidoo title also provides insight into the conflicts experienced daily by people in South Africa, and Hunt's book does the same for the Civil War era. Hinojosa's interviews provide insights into the very real nature of the conflicts today's urban teenagers face, and Patent's text describes conflicts between our desire for control over the environment and our concern for the effects of acting on that desire. Wolff's LaVaughn and Harper Lee's Scout both recognize the ways in which society can dampen an individual's spirits to the point that they lose the will to take a personal stand. Marie Lee, Miklowitz, and Namioka describe young people in conflict with the values and lifestyles of their elders, while Strasser's book is, in part, about gender conflicts.

There are both nonfiction and fiction options available, and characters reflective of the cultural diversity of the world are represented in this list. Some of the titles are more appropriate for more mature and more sophisticated readers, such as those by Strasser and Marie Lee, while others, such as Wolff's and Naidoo's, are accessible to most middle school students. Again, my point is that the options available should provide enough diversity so that all students can be successful and interested in their reading selections.

The initial purpose for reading will relate to the hypothesis. Students will be working through their class text and reading on their own to find evidence of various sorts that either supports or refutes the hypothesis. This approach is based on the "Social Inquiry" model of teaching as described thoroughly in Joyce and Weil's *Models of Teaching* (1980). The first step in the model is "orientation," or the provision of enough background information to students so that they (a) are motivated to participate, and (b) have a starting point for the inquiry.

Rather than starting from the students' own experiences, the teacher could also orient them toward the concept of conflict by asking them to collect, in advance, articles from newspapers and magazines that illustrate conflict and confrontation. Another option I have witnessed a teacher use is to invite two speakers, one reflecting each side of a hot topic, such as gun control legislation, to debate before the class, thereby illustrating "conflict." Or, *students* might debate an issue of importance to them as citizens of their particular school. Still, the end result will be that students will have a hypothesis that will help guide their reading as the unit unfolds. According to Massialas and Cox (1966), this approach has as its goal the improvement of society through the "active reconstruction" of the culture by citizens—students—taught to reflect on their values and to work with others toward a common vision.

For the two weeks following the orientation, students will read, discuss, and write about *Gulf* in class while they read their individual choice at home. While reading on their own, they are instructed to keep track of the conflict within their book in four different ways. They note:

1. incidents that illustrate different types of conflict they categorized initially;
2. incidents of conflict essential to the plot development;
3. incidents of conflict that contribute to character change/growth;
4. incidents of conflict that support or refute the class hypothesis.

It is entirely possible that any one example might fall into several of these four categories. When they finish their book, they write a paper analyzing the importance of conflict within it, using their notes as data.

In class, while moving through *Gulf,* the teacher may have to engage in some development of background knowledge. Westall is a British author, and some of the language and references in the text reflect his nationality. For example, the use of words like "Mum," and "Panda" for police cruiser, and "ice lolly" instead of Popsicle; or the references to rugby and grammar schools; and even the sentence structure reflect that Westall is British. Students can keep track of these clues as they read, using context clues and resources from the library to ensure comprehension.

Additionally, Tom and Figgis' family travel to North Wales and France and Spain, and they visit villas, castles, and other culturally based architectural structures. Westall makes references to the Ibo people of Nigeria, to "cultural attachés," to British newspapers like the *Guardian* and the *Observer.* I would do some map work or bring in copies of the papers for comparison to major U.S. papers as preparation for the reading of sections in which these references occur. Of course, students will need to know or find out about Saddam Hussein and about U.S. relations with Britain before, during, and after the Gulf crisis. They will need to know or learn about the time line of events leading up to the crisis and about what actually happened as the crisis unfolded so they understand the passages taken from new reports that described the efforts on a given day of the Allied Forces or the response to them of the Iraqi militia.

The book divides nicely into several sections. The first four chapters provide information about the family context, with foreshadowing of the problems Figgis will eventually face. As students read these chapters, they might make character charts on which they note information about the two brothers and the parents, generalizing about their personalities and making predictions about future plot events and conflicts based on this information.

Chapter 5 begins "It started that August . . ." Students can discuss why the author used the rather ambiguous "it"—a pronoun with no referent—in this sentence, and can predict what "it" will turn out to be. They should continue to complete their character charts as they read the next section, through the end of Chapter 9. It might be helpful to create a time line of events in Figgis's life and to attempt to fill it in as well with events happening in the Gulf area. As the parents react to the information—or lack thereof—they hear on the news, their different political beliefs begin to become apparent; the mother wants to shut off the radio, wants to shut out the war, while the father wants to know exactly what is going on.

[Mother said,] "A lot of people are going to get killed. Because the world is run by *men*! Mrs. Simpson's lad's out there. I had her in tears this morning, in the post office."

"I know what they're going to call this," said Dad. "The crying war. Remember when those two Aussie frigates sailed for the Gulf? It wasn't just the sailors' wives crying. It was the flippin' sailors as well. The whole world's gone soft. . . . How do you think our parents coped in World War II? When my father went to Korea, my mother didn't twitch a muscle. She cried in *private*."

"So we do nothing? And let our lads get killed for *nothing*?" (49)

They go on to talk about the fact that Iraq has the atomic bomb. The father would prefer to fight, possibly losing thousands of men now, than to risk losing millions of civilian lives through the use of the bomb. The mother cannot agree; she focuses on the fact that each of the potential thousands of men lost are individuals, with names, families, dreams, and lives of their own. She asks how he would feel if he or Tom, their son, were to be called to fight.

My father's face went as still as a stone. "I hope I would do my duty," he said coldly. . . .

"It won't be our lads that'll get killed. We'll bomb them to bits before we send our lads in. That Schwarzkopf knows what he's doing."

"Bomb them to bits?" Mum went up like a rocket again. "Don't you think the Iraqi soldiers have mothers as well? Or do you think they're made out of metal, like Daleks?" (49–50)

Students may want to take the two sides of the argument initiated in this dialogue and debate it further. They may want to consider why Westall chose to show so clearly the parents' opposing points of view. They may predict how each parent will—or will not—change as the drama continues to unfold. It is interesting to see whether the majority of the females in the class side with the mother while the majority of the males side with the father, thus introducing the idea of gender and its effect on response to the world and on communication patterns after reading this segment. Do men and women differ in the way they structure arguments and respond to conflict? What other evidence might be useful in answering this question? The teacher can video- or audiotape class discussions as a data source, and students can add this question to their "purposes for reading" as they move through their independent reading selections.

Because in this section of the text there are so many references that students may not understand, because the internal conflicts Figgis and Tom experience are tied up with the war, and because the parents experience conflicting emotions as they both anticipate England's entry into the war while watching their youngest son become increasingly distant, *Gulf* lends itself very well to the use of student-generated questions. They can discuss their questions either in small groups or in writing, by passing questions to others in the class and receiving answers, which then may spark new questions. Or, they might each write one critical question on an index card, which, collected by the teacher and pulled randomly from a hat, becomes the basis for a discussion with the entire class. Finally, when I use this strategy, I direct students to generate questions that they can answer only by using the resources of teachers of disciplines other than English, or I ask questions of them that force them into other modes of thought. For this particular unit, questions such as the following might be posed: "What would an historian/archaeologist infer about our culture if this book were discovered intact in a time capsule opened 2000 years from now?" or, "What contribution might a psychologist—or a physical educator, an artist—make to our understanding of this novel?" or "What else, besides algebra, did the Arabs contribute to the field of mathematics?"

Chapters 10 through 13 describe the process by which Figgis is medically evaluated, hospitalized, and treated, first by regular doctors, and eventually in a psychiatric institution. Chapters 14 through 16 describe Figgis' "return"—his apparent recovery and Tom's reaction to the "new" Figgis. Again, continuing to add information to both the character charts and to the time line will help students organize and process the information Westall provides. Discussion will focus now on rising tensions—in the Gulf, within Tom's family, within Tom. On the other hand, Figgis, now only responding to the world as "Latif," a thirteen-year-old soldier in an armored brigade of the Iraqi army, and speaking—most miraculously of all—only Arabic, is calm, devoid of the internal conflicts that plagued him when he waffled between two personalities.

It turns out to be Tom's story that Westall is telling. Tom has a long conversation with Dr. Rashid, who is confident enough as a doctor to be able to admit when he is mystified by the human mind; he tells Tom he cannot label Figgis "mad." Rather, Dr. Rashid prefers to think of Figgis as suffering from one of nature's many mysteries. From Rashid, Tom learns why Latif and other Iraqis hate the Americans so much. Rashid tells him that Latif and his colleagues fear the American desire to "eat up" the world's resources and that they hope Saddam Hussein will be able to halt the American appetite for more and more material goods, especially for those goods created from resources belonging to the Iraqi people. From Latif's perspective, those who have fought the Americans in the past—Japan, Germany, Vietnam— now are American puppets. Latif

> talks of San Salvador and Nicaragua . . . to 'Latif' the Americans are ravening monsters, who know no God but greed. . . . He says the British are the Americans' little dog, which barks when its master tells it to. (76)

Tom says the Iraqis are crazy to fight the world because they have no chance of winning; Rashid reminds Tom of the difficulties the Allies faced against Germany in WWII. Tom still cannot understand Latif's perspective. But Rashid can, and because he is someone Tom likes and trusts, his words, coming from his heart, finally reach into Tom's own. Rashid says he knows how they feel; he, too, has been subjected to racial slurs. Earlier in the novel, Tom's peers hurl the term "Wog poofter" at Rashid, and Rashid notes that, after several such incidents, he has felt that being dead would, perhaps, be better than to continue to be known only as a "Wog poofter." Rashid tells Tom

> Once the Arabs had a great empire, that stretched from India to the Atlantic. They were the first scientists. 'Algebra' is an Arabic word. Your maths are done with Arabic numerals. . . . You wanted to kill this Jason Bratt, because he called me a Wog poofter. Suppose you and your father and your grandfather had been called that? For generations. Would you kill then? . . . He [Saddam Hussein] is an Arab who has shaken the world. They would forgive him anything but that. (76)

When Tom reports, in the opening line of Chapter 14, "I saw things differently after that," hopefully the reader has gained some fresh insights about "the other side" as well. Perhaps through reading the novel, the students will experience some internal conflicts, the result of testing existing knowledge and belief against new information, so that they change along with Tom.

Latif, in the end, is killed. Figgis comes back to "normal," and he never again has a "thing." Tom, however, is the one whose conscience develops as a result of the events of the story, and Westall's craftsmanship in portraying the ways in which the conflict affects Tom, challenges him, and makes him grow, will be an important element in the discussion. For instance, by the time the reader reaches the end of the novel, he or she should better appreciate Westall's decision to tell the story from Tom's point of view, rather than from that of Figgis or his parents.

The teacher can guide students through the writing of a similar personal narrative in which they chronicle how dealing with some sort of conflict resulted in personal growth. Students might be given the following set of options:

1. Create a fictional story in which the main character experiences conflict that contributes to his or her personal growth and maturity. Describe within the story how the conflict was resolved. Like Westall, you may choose to mirror internal conflict in external ones.

**2.** Tell an autobiographical story in which you, as the main character, experience some sort of personal growth as a result of dealing with some sort of conflict in your world. Let the reader know how you coped with and resolved the conflict and how the experience changed you in some way.

I have found that providing the option to write fiction or nonfiction helps middle level students feel the comfort level necessary for good writing to occur; even though they are egocentric, they are often embarrassed by self-disclosure.

## Extension Through Additional Literature

Once the whole class has finished reading and processing *Gulf*, the students begin to work in small groups to extend the discussion of issues related to conflict, using their independently read titles as resources. First, those students who read the same title meet to ensure they have all understood the text on a literal level, to share responses, and to answer questions for each other about meaning. They create, as a group, a chart outlining the examples of kinds of conflict they collectively view as important within their text. Each chart will include examples of (a) incidents that illustrate the different kinds of conflict they categorized after their initial webbing session; (b) incidents of conflict essential to the plot development; (c) incidents of conflict that contribute to character change/growth; and (d) incidents of conflict that support or refute the class hypothesis. Additionally, the groups can note on their charts any responses to the text that seem to be evidence of gender differences.

Groups select a reporter who shares the group findings with the entire class. Most of the recommended additional titles for this unit have female protagonists; the exceptions are the fictional titles by Hunt and Strasser, and the nonfiction work by Hinojosa, in which the majority of the gang members interviewed are male. Therefore, it may be possible for the class to generalize about the kinds of conflicts presented as significant to male and female characters, about gender differences in response to the texts, or about gender differences in conflict resolution. I recommend Appleby and McCracken's *Gender Issues in the Teaching of English* (1992) as a source of information and ideas for teachers whose students seem interested in exploring the conflict and confrontation through the lens of gender studies. My graduate students tell me that McCracken's essay, titled "Re-Gendering the Reading of Literature" (55–68), and Bowman's "Gender Differences in Response to Literature" (80–92) in the Appleby and

McCracken book, are particularly valuable for them, especially if they are new to this approach.

Now students regroup so that, within each new group, there are representative readers for various titles. Their immediate task is to generate information—details and text examples—that will allow them to answer two questions: How is conflict related to plot and character development within a literary work? Given these literary examples, how does the setting in which a conflict occurs affect the conflict resolution process? They now use their answers to these questions to guide their reading of each other's narratives, responding to issues of plot, character, and setting with new insight as a result of their discussions.

The next task the groups undertake is to generate a list of procedures for resolving conflict, and a list of resources they might tap if a conflict seems too much for them to handle independently. Ideally, as part of the preparation for engaging in this task, the whole class should participate in an outdoor education experience designed to enhance team spirit and to allow practice of cooperation and conflict resolution skills. If there is no outdoor education center available, the help of the physical education teacher can be sought, and students can engage in trust-building and team-building activities in the gym. Or the teacher can use exercises described by researchers such as Slavin (1986; Slavin et al. 1985) within the classroom.

The students may need these conflict resolution skills as they now work together to determine the nature of the product they want to display at the "Conflict and Confrontation" fair. If the English language arts teacher has been working on this unit alone, the fair can be used to provide a forum for students to extend their investigation into the nature of conflict across disciplinary boundaries. Different groups of students will decide to explore the different sets of questions listed below in "Transdisciplinary Connections."

If a team of teachers has been working on conflict collaboratively for several weeks with students, so that they already have a transdisciplinary perspective, the fair provides an opportunity to the students to investigate questions that have arisen further, using their reading, writing, and research skills to learn more about topics that have grabbed their attention. In Chapter 5, a list of possible "products" is provided.

After the fair, to which family members, other teachers, and other students are invited, the class revisits the initial hypothesis. At this point, they may decide that they have, to their satisfaction, "proven" it. They may decide it needs to be revised based on their accumulated knowledge base. Or, they may decide they need even more information—and their inquiring minds take off in a new direction, leading them into a study of a specific conflict between peoples, such as the Holocaust, or into the investigation of how conflicts are resolved in specific settings, such as the corporate world, or into the exploration of some topic only tangentially related to conflict, such as the hole in the ozone and its effect on the food chain and global warming. Maybe they will decide they want to participate in peer mediation training and establish a peer mediation program in their school. If the students have been actively engaged in this unit, if they have felt some ownership and responsibility for their own learning, it is very likely that they will want to continue learning, and the teachers will have to follow their lead to see where their quest for knowledge takes them next.

## Transdisciplinary Connections

The transdisciplinary connections for "Conflict and Confrontation" may arise naturally from Westall's text. The centrality of the Persian Gulf War to Tom's story provides an excellent starting point for inquiry into other cultures, their values, history, religion, views on women and children, laws, and customs. Learning about the geography, topology, climate, and wildlife of the region allows for exploration of science concepts, and the role of the Arabic world in the history of mathematics can also be investigated. Infusing study of the art, music, dance, and social customs, including sports, of Iraq and Kuwait and of other Arab countries will enrich students' understanding of the text, as will study of the architecture and art Tom mentions visiting as a tourist in France, Spain, and northern Wales. The term *schizophrenia* is mentioned as one possible diagnosis for Figgis, though Dr. Rashid rejects it; mental illness, stress, the way the brain functions might all be discussed, allowing the health teacher to enhance and expand the knowledge base students bring to bear upon the text. Of course, since the author is British and the book takes place in England, there are many topics related to U.S./British relationships and to cultural differences and similarities that can be investigated as well.

If the overall goal of the unit is that students will increase their understanding of the nature of conflict and its role in everyday life, however, then I believe that the transdisciplinary experiences should help them move beyond the boundaries of the literary world in which they are immersed as they read *Gulf*.

1. Sample unit question: What is the role of conflict in everyday life?
2. Sample focusing questions for generating discipline-based problems: What are the component elements of conflict? Is conflict useful or is it always a negative force? How is conflict resolved?

What are the relationships among conflict, confrontation, compromise, and consensus?

3. What are some sample disciplinary questions and tasks related to question #2?

   a. *Math:* How are statistics manipulated during times of conflict? What are the pros and cons of various number systems, and how and why did the Arabic system become more accepted than the Roman numeral system? How do we use mathematical concepts to resolve conflicts in daily life? Task: Make a scrapbook of newspaper and popular press articles that demonstrate the use of math to deal with daily conflict; write captions, an introduction, and a concluding analysis of findings. A useful resource for integrating the use of computer technology into the math component of a unit on "Conflict and Confrontation" is an article by Alterman (1992), "The Number 2 Challenge," which details his use of computer responses to generate conflict within his students, prompting them to search for more creative and alternative solutions to specific problems.

   b. *Science:* What conflicts exist in the natural worlds— botanical, geological, zoological, chemical—and how are these resolved? Is compromise evident in the natural world, or does one force always achieve dominance when two forces collide? In what ways are the desires of humankind for a comfortable, controlled environment in conflict with the laws of nature? What happens when the laws of nature are broken? Task: Create a videotape or other media presentation that shows examples of conflict in the natural world with a text articulating the categories of conflict illustrated and the lessons we can learn from them.

   c. *Social studies:* How do the value systems and belief structures of various cultures affect their ability to resolve conflict? Historically, what strategies have been used to resolve conflicts between groups of people with differing belief systems, and what lessons, if any, can we learn from these examples? What are the "hot spots" in today's global community, and what might be done to defuse their potential for global destruction? Within the United States, what conflicting belief structures exist and how can we live peacefully given those differences? Task: Research a current "hot spot." As the ambassador from that country, seek audience with the President of the United States (a part to be played by the teacher, with other students as "presidential advisors"), explaining your country's point of view and asking for the United States to fill whatever role you believe to be appropriate in your affairs.

d.  *Language arts:* What conflicts indicative of various cultures', periods', or authors' values are evident in related literary texts? How does conflict advance plot? What is the potential role of story in interpersonal conflict resolution? Task: With a partner, write a dialogue between two characters from two different books explaining how they deal with conflict, how their approach to conflict has been influenced by their personal experiences (in the world of the text) and by the cultural context in which that text was written; perform the dialogue "in role."

e.  *Health:* How do various cultures describe and deal with the internal conflicts that result in stress and mental illness? What strategies are personally useful for alleviating internal conflict? Task: Analyze the personal stress level and the causes of stress within your life, then create a plan for stress reduction; follow the plan for at least two weeks and analyze the results.

f.  *Physical education:* What is the role of conflict in sport? How are these conflicts resolved? What lessons can we learn from the world of athletics about conflict resolution that might assist in conflict resolution in other contexts? How is conflict ritualized in other cultures? Again, what lessons can be learned from these ritual confrontations for conflict resolution in daily life? Task: Participate in two different team sports on a regular basis for three weeks during P.E. Keep a journal of reactions to these experiences, writing a culminating entry about your ability and motivation to play given the nature of the conflicts involved.

g.  *Art:* What role does an artist's internal conflict play in his or her artistic process? How does an artist create conflict in the viewer? How is conflict used to arouse the viewer's interest?

h. *Music:* What "conflicts" exist from a musical theory
perspective and what is the role of such "conflicts" in
the musician's effort to arouse a listener's response?
(For instance, how is the listener affected when a
chord progression or a harmony violates expectations?) How do musicians reflect the conflict of the
cultural context in which they compose and perform
in their work? Task: Listen to several representative
pieces from each of several periods in music history to
find examples of conflict and conflict resolution.

Toward the end of *Make Lemonade* by Virginia Euwer Wolff,
LaVaughn, the thirteen-year-old narrator, recounts a dialogue
between herself and Jolly, a seventeen-year-old mother of two, who,
in large part due to LaVaughn's intervention, is finally finding the
tools she needs to get herself out of the hole of poverty in which she
has been living. Jolly is telling LaVaughn a story which has had a pro-
found effect on her. In the story, a blind woman with enough money
to purchase "the one best orange" from a fruit market for her starving
children, discovers she has been tricked. She is taking home a sour
lemon instead. Jolly points out that this is a fairly common occurrence
in her life's experience, noting that most of the time she even *thanks*
the person who gave her the lemon:

"See how they get you when you're down,
you don't even know it's a lemon."
She's building up steam, this Jolly is.
"You even *thank* them for it,
and you go stumblin' home,
all bleeding or however you're hurt—
and you say to yourself,
  'Well, gosh, I guess somebody give me a lemon.
  Ain't I stupid.
  Ain't I dumb. I must've deserved it
  if I was so stupid not to know."

And Jolly looks at me,
angry because she understands.

"So. This is the next part of the story. Guess what
the blind woman does next.
"Guess," she goes on at me.
This Jolly she's excited now.

I tell Jolly I don't know. I say
"Her children are all hungry, she's blind,
she'd got just this one lemon,

I don't even like this story, Jolly.
Why're you telling it?"

"For the *point* of it," she says.
"You know what she does next?
She finds this little teensy bit of old caked, lumpy sugar
she had packed away, and she mixes it up
with the juice of the lemon
and some clean water from the spring they have there,
and she makes lemonade.
And she feeds it to her starving little ones.
And that's the end of the story.
That's the point of it."
And I get the point of it this time.

And I want to put my arms all the way around Jolly
in congratulation
and I'm happy she's so angry
and I'm proud of her
she made it clearer than my Mom ever did
with all the preaching and huffing
and bootstraps.

But I hold back. I don't go hugging Jolly.
She's too angry to hug.
It's like some bricks got fit in the wall
where it was crumbly before. (172–73)

Jolly, through this story, has made sense of many of the conflicts, both internal and external, that have kept her paralyzed, and through sharing the story with LaVaughn, she has begun to resolve some of the conflicts within their relationship. Through transdisciplinary study centered on a literary text written for young adults, middle level students may experience a safe haven in which to explore the multiple conflicts that are synonymous with adolescence, and, like Jolly from *Make Lemonade*, and Tom from *Gulf*, learn tools for dealing with conflict that they can carry with them throughout their lives.

## Works Cited

Appleby, Bruce C., and Nancy Mellin McCracken, eds. 1992. *Gender Issues in the Teaching of English*. Portsmouth, NH: Boynton/Cook.

Alterman, Alan E. 1992. "The Number 2 Challenge." *Arithmetic Teacher* 40(3): 180–82.

Bettendorf, Joline. 1987. *Literature of War and Peace. Section II: Survival and Afterward*. ERIC Document ED370816.

Bowman, Cynthia. 1992. "Gender Diffferences in Response to Literature." In

*Gender Issues in the Teaching of English,* edited by Bruce Appleby and Nancy McCracken. Portsmouth, NH: Boynton/Cook.

Cowen, Gregory, and Elizabeth Cowen. 1980. *Writing.* Glenview, IL: Scott, Foresman and Company.

Huhtala, Jack. 1994. "Group Investigation: Structuring an Inquiry-Based Curriculum." Paper presented at the Annual Meeting of the American Educational Research Association, New Orleans, April 4–8. ERIC Document ED373050.

Joyce, B., and M. Weil. 1980. *Models of Teaching.* 2d ed. Englewood Cliffs, NJ: Prentice Hall.

Kennemer, Phyllis K. 1994. *Using Literature to Teach Middle Grades About War.* ERIC Document ED364494.

Massialas, Byron, and Benjamin Cox. 1966. *Inquiry in the Social Studies.* New York: McGraw Hill.

McCracken, Nancy. 1992. "Re-Gendering the Reading of Literature." In *Gender Issues in the Teaching of English,* edited by Bruce Appleby and Nancy McCracken. Portsmouth, NH: Boynton/Cook.

Slavin, R. E. 1986. *Student Team Learning: An Overview and Practical Guide.* Washington, D.C.: National Education Association.

Slavin, R. E., Sharon Shlomo, Spencer Kagan, Rachel Lazarountz, Clark Webb, and Richard Schmuch, eds. 1985. *Learning to Cooperate, Cooperating to Learn.* New York: Plenum Press.

Westall, Robert. 1992. *Gulf.* London: Metheun Children's Books.

Wolff, Virginia Euwer. 1994. *Make Lemonade.* New York: Scholastic.

# Four

# Surviving, Living, and Disturbing the Universe

When I conducted a survey of 339 middle school students as to their level of interest in the concepts put forward by middle school experts as being appropriate for transdisciplinary study by young adolescents, survival received the second highest mean score, a 3.982. Exploration, power, and freedom ranked respectively a very close third, fourth, and fifth (3.819; 3.769; and 3.714); these three concepts relate to survival in many ways, and taken together, provide insight into the problems that interest middle level students.

I found it telling that one young man, an eighth grader from a fairly affluent school suffering from tensions between its strong Jewish population and its steadily increasing African American population, condemned the entire survey. He wrote, after rating survival as 5, power as 5, exploration as 5, and freedom as 5, "I and others might be interested in some topics that are more interesting and exciting [than the ones on the survey]. Social issues that the class wants to discuss, such as drugs, sex, violence, pollution, school, abortion, guns, racism, child abuse, crime, gay rights, prostitution, homicide, disease, strikes, date rapes, suicide, things like that. That's what you need for your book, not change, extinction, culture, energy. The youth of today want to know about the world, about conflicts, and views. Thank you. Help us to survive out of school!" This young man recognizes, as do so many middle school students, that surviving already is a complicated process, and that it will become increasingly difficult over time.

# Rationale

How many times do we tell students that what they learn in school is necessary for survival? Most curricula are designed to some degree to help students prepare for life outside the relatively safe, structured environment of school. Demands for additions to the curriculum—such as those made for more structured, explicit attention to technological literacy, and to service learning—are frequently made based on the necessity for students' future survival. When budgets are tightened at the elementary level, music and art teachers frequently are eliminated because these are not considered "core" or "essential" subject areas. When the state of Maryland decided to create a new set of school assessment procedures—calling for students to work in small groups to solve real-life problems that required the synthesis of skills drawn from multiple content areas—the rationale was that such assessments better reflect the survival demands of today's society than do more traditional, individual competency tests of basic skill and knowledge.

Survival, then, is a concept of importance to society in general and to teachers and students in particular. It is a concept invoked when curricular and instructional decisions are made.

Perhaps more important, "just" surviving seems to be one of the primary goals of middle school students. I recall the many tears shed as my middle grade students struggled to survive during their first year in middle school, the difficult switch from having one teacher in one room for the bulk of the day to moving from classroom to classroom, teacher to teacher. I found it almost painful to watch them trying to survive living inside a changing body—and, even worse, trying to survive the cliquishness, a result of their insecurity, of middle school social life.

My students were eloquent in expressing the difficulties inherent in trying to survive being "in between." Considered too young for the sophisticated level of social activity many of them crave—including dating, working, and generally increasing distance from identification with the family—they are considered too old for the displays of anger, tears, and extreme emotion that so often rage inside them, or for the concern over the personal imperfections they feel so keenly, and for the lack of patience and cooperation they often exhibit as they attempt to move toward independence. They have to survive their growing awareness of their differences. At the middle school level, students are cognitively sophisticated enough to realize the ways in which they are different from their peers—often painfully so—without recognizing that these very differences are what make them special and unique. Here is Lisa, from *Commander Coatrack Returns* (McNair 1989), describing herself at age thirteen:

I'm pretty much a nothing at school just because I'm smart. Hey, I'm not a genius or anything, but when I get called on to answer a question in class I get it right often enough to get ribbed by kids. I probably would get picked on less if I ribbed them back, but instead I always blush and get tongue-tied and turn away. That sort of behavior has not only got me labeled as a brain but as a brain who's a snob. And nobody is attracted to someone who's a brain and a snob and who also rates about a −4 on the beauty scale. (14)

Eventually, Lisa will learn to accept her abilities and will use them to her advantage as she pursues her desired career (already, at age thirteen, she thinks she wants to be an astronaut), but in the meantime, she has to survive the ins and outs of middle school day by day. Thus, it is not surprising that middle level students are interested in studying survival, a process that is *the* goal of their daily lives—especially if surviving in school turns out to be less difficult than surviving the problems of abuse, neglect, alcohol and drug addiction, homelessness, or disease that trouble so many of the youth in today's world.

Finally, middle school students who are beginning to engage in formal operational thinking therefore often begin to have a sense of the discrepancies between the real world in which they live and other, more ideal worlds they can conceptualize. They often perceive the hypocrisy of adults and the ills of the world around them with despair, so that it is important for them to develop a belief in each individual's ability to contribute to changing the status quo. Bill, a friend of the main character in *Footprints in the Water* by Phyllis Reynolds Naylor (1981), expresses this point very clearly. He and Dan have been talking about the possibility of nuclear war. Bill says,

And today, we still think in terms of war or surrender. If you can't work things out at the conference table, you fight. If you're not top dog, number one, you're going to end up slaves. People just accept that this is true. I don't think it is. We need a new explorer to come up with alternatives.

He goes on to say he writes for the school newspaper as its editor and for the local paper through letters to its editor because:

It makes me feel I'm doing *something*, that's all. That's the only way I can deal with it. *Do* something. Get involved. Even if the chances are small, at least I'll know I was one of the ones who tried. That's what keeps me going. (33–34)

## Unit Goals

The specific contexts in which this unit are taught will lead the teachers involved to add or subtract goals as appropriate. In general, speaking, listening, reading, writing, thinking, and socialization skills should be incorporated. Also, depending on the degree of student ownership of this unit as the result of inquiry-based teaching, students may generate questions that lead them into deleting some goals while adding others. As a starting point, the unit presented in these pages should allow students to be able to

1. Define "survival" and describe the knowledge and skills necessary for survival in diverse circumstances based on personal experiences, experiences with a literary text, and information gathered through transdisciplinary study.

2. Describe the relationship between the concept of survival as a literary theme, and the plot development, setting, and characterization.

3. Generalize about the personal characteristics necessary for survival in any set of circumstances and self-evaluate based on this list of character traits.

4. Compare and contrast literary texts sharing the theme of survival.

5. Compare and contrast the ways in which survival is treated in fictional and nonfictional works.

6. Research the concept of survival from a variety of discipline-based perspectives, including research from the scientific and medical communities about survival needs, from primary source material and fiction about ways in which both individuals and groups of people have survived in diverse cultural and geographic settings, and from interviews with practicing members of the work force about math skills necessary for daily survival on the job.

7. Generalize about the differences, if any, between "surviving" and "living."

8. Synthesize unit content in a personally meaningful way through both individual and group presentations/performances.

## Annotations of the Text Set

In this unit, students will each read one title from three different groups of titles. Each set of options deals with a different kind of survival. The first set of titles are all "traditional" survival titles; in each one, a young person (or persons) has to survive in a harsh, difficult environment. In the second set of titles, the theme of survival is present, but the young person is attempting to survive in difficult emotional circumstances, rather than having to concentrate on staying alive. In the third set of titles, the main characters have to make choices between merely surviving or maintaining the status quo, and disturbing their universe in order to create a more meaningful life for themselves and others.

I would organize these titles into sets of three, one title from each of the three categories. Students then choose which set they prefer to read. Thus, as teacher, I would be able to organize both "expert" and "jigsaw" groups for discussion purposes both during the reading of the novels and after completion of the reading, and will have groups of students in place who have shared the experience of reading the same three titles when it is time for them to create a final project. If none of the following titles seems appropriate, Lindberg's 1974 annotated bibliography describes sixty older survival tales of various types, and Speare (1988) examines the elements basic to the survival story genre. The annotations from Appendix B could be tapped by teachers and students looking for just the right book for this unit, as could the resources outlined.

## Tales of Physical Survival

**Cole, Brock. 1987. *The Goats*. New York: Farrar, Straus, Giroux.**

A boy and a girl, labeled "the goats" because they are the camp's misfits, must work together to survive after the other campers strip them and abandon them on an island as a prank.

**Hobbs, Will. 1991. *Downriver*. New York: Atheneum.**

When Jesse and her companions steal their counselor's van to go white-water rafting through the Grand Canyon on their own, these troubled teenagers have more of an adventure than they had planned.

**Klein, Gerda Weissman. 1995. *All but My Life*. New York: Hill and Wang (Farrar, Straus, Giroux).**

Of the four thousand slave girls forced on a thousand-mile winter march from one concentration camp to another, Gerda Weissman was one of only two hundred slave girls who survived, only to realize the Nazis had taken all but her life. In this remarkable document of the triumph of the human spirit and will to love, Klein recounts her story, one of hope and faith and even kindness in the midst of incredible destruction, cruelty, and violence. (The chapter "Anne Frank's *The Diary of a Young Girl*: World War II and "Young Adult Literature" by Joan Kaywell (1993b), in *Adolescent Literature as a Complement to the Classics* provides an excellent overview of other titles about survival in WWII.)

**Paulsen, Gary. 1987. *Hatchet*. New York: Bradbury.**

Brian, the lone survivor of a plane crash in the Canadian wilderness, learns how to fight the elements and, in the process, learns how to fight against the rage that has filled him.

**Sebestyen, Ouida. 1988. *The Girl in the Box*. Boston: Little Brown (Joy Street Books).**

Jackie McGee has been kidnapped and locked in a deep, dark hole; she survives on very little food and water and maintains her spirits by writing a series of notes—the body of this text—on a typewriter she happens to have with her when abducted.

**Taylor, Theodore. 1994. *Sweet Friday Island*. New York: Harcourt Brace.**

On vacation, Peg Toland and her father discover that their camping expedition to an uninhabited island in the Sea of Cortez has landed them in a deadly trap.

**Wartski, Maureen Crane. 1980. *A Boat to Nowhere*. New York: Signet.**

Fourteen-year-old orphan Kien, Mai, her grandfather, and her little brother take the desperate risk of becoming boat people rather than remain in a Vietnam filled with terrible conquerors.

The titles above include both fiction and nonfiction. Some are fairly easy to read, such as *The Goats* and *Hatchet*; others require more sophisticated reading skills, such as the Klein title. The clash between cultures is an issue in both the Klein autobiography and the Wartski novel. *Hatchet* has a male protagonist, *The Girl in the Box*, a female. The other titles have both male and females as main characters. Teachers who would like additional options, including poetry, science fiction, and other genres might investigate the titles annotated in Appendix B.

### *Tales of Survival During Emotional Crisis*

**Crutcher, Chris. 1993. *Staying Fat for Sarah Byrnes*. New York: Greenwillow.**

Sarah, victim of child abuse, finally leaves her father's house, seeking refuge in a mental hospital. She eventually moves on with her life with the help of her friend in this tale of courage, loyalty, and love touched with a rather "black" sense of humor.

**Irwin, Hadley. 1985.** *Abby, My Love.* **New York: Atheneum (Margaret K. McElderry).**

Chip and Abby have a loving relationship filled with humor and tenderness, but it is challenged when Abby finally reveals that her father has been sexually abusing her for years.

**Powell, Randy. 1995.** *Dean Duffy.* **New York: Farrar, Straus, Giroux.**

Having once achieved stardom as the pitcher for the American team that defeated Cuba and as a hitter with a grand-slam homer of 507 feet, Dean Duffy plummets into a slump that lasts through his senior year. When he graduates, he is confused about who he is, about what he wants from the future, and about what, if anything, he can do to take charge of his life.

**O'Dell, Scott. 1990.** *My Name Is Not Angelica.* **New York: Dell/ Yearling.**

Sixteen-year-old Raisha and her betrothed, Konje, an African tribal chief, are captured and sold into slavery. After surviving an arduous journey to the West Indies, Konje escapes and becomes the leader of a group of runaways planning revolt. Raisha, called Angelica by her master, has to decide what her own fate will be.

**Oneal, Zibby. 1980.** *The Language of Goldfish.* **New York: Viking.**

Growing up seems to be harder for Carrie Stokes, now thirteen, than it is for her classmates, and when her family moves to the suburbs, and all the changes in her life seem to be more than she can bear, this artistically talented young woman is almost ready to give up on life.

**Rochman, Hazel, ed. 1988.** *Somehow Tenderness Survives: Stories of Southern Africa.* **New York: HarperKeypoint.**

The ten stories in this collection, some autobiographical, reflect the ways in which the practice of apartheid causes suffering for those living in its shadow, regardless of their race.

**Woodson, Jacqueline. 1994.** *I Hadn't Meant to Tell You This.* **New York: Delacorte.**

For Marie, popular leader of her Black peers, Lena's secret about the ways her father treats her and her little sister, now that their mother has died, seems too much to bear. She struggles to determine how she can best help her friend. Should she keep quiet and let Lena go? Should she tell someone? The language and complexity of this story of race and friendship, of power and loss are compelling; Marie manages to express the insights she achieves through her relationship with Lena and her new understanding of her absent mother without seeming older than her years.

## Surviving While Daring to Disturb the Universe

**Beake, Leslie. 1993.** *Song of Be.* **New York: Henry Holt.**

Be, now an adolescent, longs for the peaceful life of the Kalahari Desert she recalls from her childhood as a member of a Bushman tribe, but with the help of Khu, she begins to realize that Namibia cannot go back in time, and that her generation has to fight to make a new kind of reality for all the people of the country.

**Korman, Gordon. 1985.** *Don't Care High.* **New York: Scholastic.**

In this humorous novel, Paul, who has never been the type to get involved, decides to help shake up the incredibly apathetic student body and its teachers and change the image of "Don't Care High."

**Meyer, Carolyn. 1993.** *White Lilacs.* **New York: Harcourt Brace (Gulliver Books).**

Rose Lee, a twelve-year-old living in Dillon, Texas, in 1921, is surrounded by the debate that erupts about how the Black community should respond to a decision on the part of the White community to raze "Freedomtown" and relocate its residents to an ugly, barren stretch of land outside of town. Based on the true history of Meyer's Texas town.

**Soto, Gary. 1994.** *Jesse.* **New York: Harcourt Brace.**

Jesse wants to be an artist, but a lifetime of labor in the fields seems to be the only future available to Mexican Americans—unless, as is the case for Jesse's brother Abel, being drafted and sent to Vietnam turns out to be an alternative. Soto describes with vivid detail a year in their life as, living together and struggling to support themselves while attending a community college, these two young men search for hope and try to establish a value system that will provide an anchor in an otherwise unstable social and political environment.

**Schwandt, Stephen. 1995.** *The Last Goodie.* **Minneapolis: Free Spirit Press.**

Marty Oliver, track superstar, is haunted by the unsolved disappearance twelve years earlier of his former babysitter, also a track hero. When a new lead is discovered in the case, Marty finds himself involved in uncovering the truth about Stacy, and in laying to rest the ghosts from the past that haunt him.

**Symynkywicz, Jeffrey. 1995.** *Vaclav Havel and the Velvet Revolution.* **Parsippany, NJ: Silver Burdett (Dillon).**

Vaclav Havel, a dissident playwright in Czechoslovakia, spent years fighting for freedom of expression during the Communist rule, a stand for which he was sentenced to five years of hard labor in a prison camp; eventually, he and others achieved their dream of a free, independent Czechoslovakian republic, and Havel was elected president in 1989.

**Temple, Frances. 1995.** *Tonight, by Sea.* **New York: Orchard.**

Two years after the military coup that fells Aristide's Haitian government, Paulie's uncle finds himself too busy digging graves for the victims of violence and starvation of the new military regime; he decides he cannot put off taking action any longer, and with the help of Paulie and the community, he uses his coffin-builder's skills to construct the vessel "Seek Life."

## Unit Activities

To initiate the unit, I would want to generate an awareness of the kinds of skills required for surviving on a daily basis. Thus, I would try to engage students in the practice of any one of several possible skills that they will observe literary characters using once they begin their reading. For example, acute observation is a requirement for survival in the wilderness. To help students sharpen their own observation skills, Stephanie Zenker, a Baltimore County, Maryland, English teacher, has a potato (or a carrot, peanut, etc.) on each student's desk at the beginning of the class period. The task is for each student to observe the object, without altering it, and to describe his or her potato so clearly and accurately that when the potatoes are collected and displayed en masse, not only will the "owner" be able to correctly identify it, but a partner will be able to pick it out of the group based on the written description as well.

After students write about their potatoes, and several of them attempt to pick one out of the pile based on the description, Zenker sometimes has them work in groups to revise their descriptions using compare/contrast techniques. It may prove easier to describe one potato as it relates to others in a small group; out of the group of five, John may be able to say his potato is the smallest, the darkest, the bumpiest. Then the entire class looks at all the potatoes and attempts to generalize based on their observations about the generic qualities of the potato.

When the students have engaged in as much observation, talk, and writing as seems profitable, Zenker asks them to generate a list of times during the day when observation skills are crucial for successful navigation through a given activity. Additionally or alternatively, students can list academic tasks that depend upon sharp observation skills for successful completion. Finally, a general discussion about survival skills takes place.

An alternative way into the unit might be to ask students to brainstorm the difficulties they encountered when they entered middle school/junior high, or those they anticipate facing when they move on to high school. How do they cope with these difficulties? How does having to deal with these difficulties affect their overall quality of life? What skills have they found useful or necessary for surviving in the face of these difficulties? And, how might these skills be similar to or different from those skills they would anticipate needing if faced with the prospect of enduring a physically challenging situation? The movie *Snowbound* (1977), in which a young girl and slightly older teenage boy have to survive when they are lost in a snowstorm, can then be shown; students watch the movie while listing skills and attributes that contribute to this unlikely pair's ability to survive.

In either case, as the teacher, I would try to tap the students' experience and knowledge related to the concept of survival using strategies designed to help students feel actively engaged in the learning process and recognize the real-world implications of studying about survival. Then—and this is the tricky, almost scary part of planning a unit in this fashion—with students' help, I would try to use what emerges to help them focus their reading and study during the unit.

In an ideal world, there would be enough books available for all students to have one title in hand to take home, and they would be reliable enough to complete the reading of that text on their own after the teacher has done some book-talking, any necessary vocabulary priming, and some development of background knowledge for each title. For instance, it might be useful for students to know something about the nature of the Canadian wilderness, to know where the Sea of Cortez is located, or to understand what happened in Haiti in 1989, and what the climatic conditions are in any of these places before reading. They may need some historical information before plunging into the Klein or Wartski titles.

If students can read their entire text independently at home, the teacher needs to provide some "purpose-for-reading" questions or tasks that will help them focus on those aspects of the book around which future discussion will take place. For example, as they read, students can complete a web with the main character(s) name in the middle on which they note details of setting/environment, personality traits, skills, coping mechanisms demonstrated, and conflicts encountered that make survival either likely or unlikely. Thus, when it is time for students to work with others, they have a body of information—data about survival—in hand to prompt their thinking.

However, I seldom found myself in such an ideal situation, and the student teachers with whom I work frequently find themselves in less than ideal situations. Therefore, the students may have to read their selections during class time. If this is the case, I suggest to my student teachers that they try the kind of format Joseph uses, as described in Chapter 2, "There's No Place Like Home." Each day, students read in class while also keeping a journal about their reading. The teacher and/or the students generate sentence starters to prime the pump for their writing; items such as "I am like or different from the main character because _____ "; "I predict the main character will do _____ because _____ "; "The setting is/is not important to this story because _____ "; "If the main character could change one thing about his/her situation, it would be _____ "; and "If the author could give the main character one tool—personality/character trait or physical tool—that would help that character survive more readily, it would be _____ because _____ " all help students to focus their reading.

I have observed teachers using graphic organizers such as those described by Lyman, Lopez, and Mindlus (1986), designed to facilitate students' understanding of cause-and-effect relationships in order to guide reading and comprehension regardless of whether students are reading in class or on their own time. For instance, a "chain" (Figure 4–1) can be used to track how one event leads inexorably to the next. Or a "jellyfish" (Figure 4–2) could be used to help students note how one problem might have several different possible solutions, the choice of any one of which will result in different paths of action. A "decision-making chart" (Figure 4–3) could also be kept either individually or by students all reading the same title on the specific problems facing an individual character, possible solutions, and the pros

**Figure 4–1**

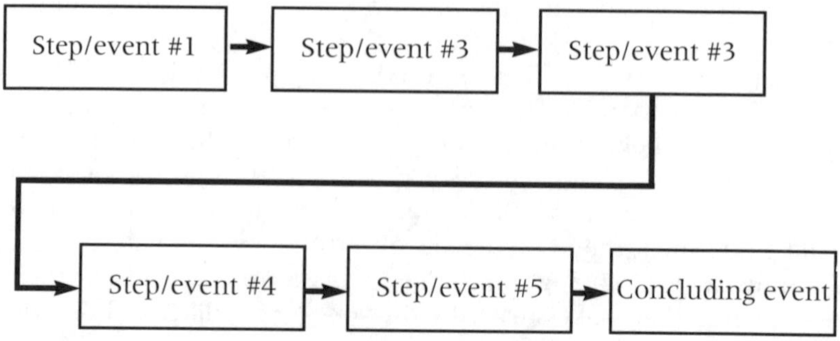

**Figure 4–2**

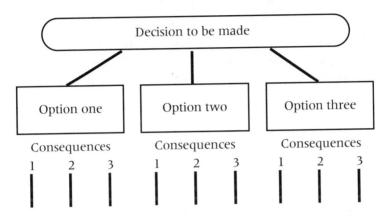

and cons of each, as well as the "reality base" for each. Or, students could work together to create visual representations of the settings in which the characters have to survive, with accompanying explanation, in order to help them better appreciate the relationship between setting and plot, especially in tales of physical survival. For additional advice on the uses of art as a response strategy, read Paley's (1988) description of a project called "Kids of Survival," involving a changing group of minority students in New York City who create art in response to their study of literature.

**Figure 4–3**

| A. Character's possible courses of action at X point in the story | Pros | Cons |
|---|---|---|
| 1. Option one - (describe) | | |
| 2. Option two - (describe) | | |
| 3. Option three - (describe) | | |
| 4. Option four - (describe) | | |

Each time students finish reading one of the different kinds of survival texts, they work first in "expert groups" with the other students who have read the title to ensure that each reader has literal comprehension of the story. In these groups, students also generate answers to such questions as:

1. Who had to survive? Was this person successful in surviving?

2. What skills did they have that contributed to their success? What skills did they initially lack that they had to develop in order to survive?

3. What personality or character traits helped them to survive?

4. How did the setting influence the kinds of skills and attributes needed for survival?

5. What kind of help, if any, did they have from other people that was necessary to their survival?

6. Did the individual ever consider an option other than survival? If so, why? If not, why not? At what point did the individual commit to a path of attempted survival? At what point was survival ensured?

7. How did you as readers react to the story? What did the author do to make you want to read? If you did not want to read, what was it about the plot, character, setting, style, or other aspects of the book that made reading difficult or detracted from motivation to read it?

8. Could you identify with any of the people in your book? How and why?

The students then work in groups composed of readers of each of the different titles in each survival category. For example, in the next group discussion about physical survival, there will be at least one reader of the Cole, Hobbs, Klein, Paulsen, Sebestyen, Taylor, and Wartski titles. Each reader will provide an overview of their title, emphasizing the survival element, and drawing upon their discussions in their expert groups. Once everyone has knowledge of all seven titles, the group attempts to generalize about the answers to several questions, including

1. What skills did the survivors in these titles have that contributed to their success? What skills did they initially lack that they had to develop in order to survive?

2. What personality or character traits helped them to survive?

3. How did the setting influence the kinds of skills and attributes needed for survival?

4. What kind of help, if any, did they have from other people that was necessary to their survival?

5. What decisions do individuals faced with difficulties of survival have to make? Do people in such situations ever consider an option other than survival? If so, why? If not, why not? What factors lead individuals trying to survive against incredible physical odds to commit to a path of attempted survival?

6. What lessons, if any, for our own daily survival can we learn from reading tales of survival against physical difficulties?

7. How did you as readers react to these stories?

8. Could you identify with any of the people in your book? How and why?

9. What seem to be the characteristics of "survival literature"?

10. Task: Write a poem using at least one significant phrase from each book represented in your group about the characteristics of "survivors."

Groups share their answers to these questions, and the class continues the process of generalizing. Now that everyone has a wealth of knowledge about survival based on their reading, the students are reorganized into groups composed of individuals who read the same three titles based on the "text sets" originally organized by the teacher. At this point, I would assign two tasks. First, they have to create some sort of visual presentation that shows the similarities among their titles. They will display these visuals and explain them to their classmates, or in some larger public forum if time permits and it seems useful to do so. Secondly, they will be responsible for generating a list of questions and possible strategies for finding answers to them that they can use as the springboard for continued investigation. The groups can either share their questions, voting as a class on which ones to explore, or each group can choose one or more to pursue. If only one content-area teacher is working with these students in isolation from teachers of other disciplines, the "Transdisciplinary Connections" can be shared with the students, who may choose from the questions and tasks posed here.

Finally, when students and teacher(s) agree that they want to move out of this unit on survival, as a class, students can either create a "survival manual" of some sort—for incoming students or for peers moving on to high school, for travelers heading to a specific country, for parents of adolescents, or for tourists visiting their area— or they might conduct a "survival night" workshop for any of the same groups. Thus they will have an opportunity to apply what they have learned to real-life situations and to communicate that knowledge to a real audience genuinely able to benefit from their growing expertise. Or, the teacher might choose to present the kind of futuristic time travel project focused on survival described by Rosenberg (1994), or a project about the survival of ghost towns, described by Van Cleaf (1993).

## Transdisciplinary Connections

Many of the titles described above should provoke student interest in topics that are traditionally studied in classrooms other than the English language arts class. Then teachers of other disciplines could build on that emerging interest. Rochman's and Beake's texts, for instance, beg the reader to learn more about the social, cultural, and political history of various African nations. I wanted to know more about the Holocaust after reading Klein's autobiography, and about the "Velvet Revolution" after reading the biography of Havel; students feeling the same way are well-poised for further investigation. Or, they may, as I did, want more information about "Boat People" after reading *Boat to Nowhere* and *Tonight, By Sea*, and about the historical realities upon which O'Dell based his novel. Research into the history of race relations in the United States might be prompted through the reading of *White Lilacs* or *Jesse*. I have observed students' interest in mental illness—its causes and treatments—become piqued from reading *The Language of Goldfish*, and Dean Duffy's involvement in baseball provided a springboard for a discussion in my methods class for future P.E. teachers both of the sport and of how talent is defined and nurtured within the field. I have watched the Woodson title prompt young adults to delve into research into child abuse and how its victims cope and what society can do to prevent it, and it seems to me the question of how writing and artistic endeavors serve as healing activities might be investigated after reading Schwandt's or Sebestyen's novels.

However, in a more transdisciplinary effort, I would envision teachers of all content areas working together to help students broaden the concept of survival that they achieve from their immersion in the texts.

1. Sample unit question: What does survival mean and what is the boundary between surviving and living?

2. Sample focusing questions for generating discipline-based problems: What are the skills required for survival in the student's daily reality? How are these skills related to those required for survival

in different contexts? Is mere survival always a worthy goal? At what point does "surviving" become "copping out?" What are the relationships among survival, power, and freedom? How is survival on one's own different from survival within a group?

3. What are some sample disciplinary questions and tasks related to question #2?

   a. *Math:* What knowledge and skills developed through the study of mathematics are essential to survival in diverse contexts and settings? Why have certain mathematical constructs survived over time, while others have been lost or pushed aside? How do mathematicians define a "powerful" mathematical theory? Task: Interview at least three adults who hold different kinds of jobs about the ways in which they use math skills and concepts in their professional lives. As part of the conclusion of the report based on these interviews, self-assess mathematical skill and describe two goals for the future as a student of math.

   b. *Science:* How have various species of life adapted to the surroundings in order to survive, and what lessons can humankind learn from them? Why did the dinosaurs and/or other creatures now extinct fail to survive, and what lessons can we learn? What are the forces that affect the survival capabilities of geological structures and geographical regions of the world (such as how a fossil is formed and then "survives" through time, or how the movement of tectonic plates affects the survival of a specific region of the world, or how the rain forests survive and regenerate if left alone)? What kinds of actions do the political leaders of today's world need to take in order to help ensure the survival of scientific inquiry and the survival of humankind? Task: Research the survival strategies of a particular creature (or of a geological/geographical construct), using all available technologies, and contribute to a collective display about "Survival in the Natural World." Based on the developing collective wisdom, write a class letter to a politician articulating advice on ecological and environmental issues of local or national significance.

   c. *Social studies:* How do groups of people survive under various climatic, geographical, and societal conditions? What knowledge and skills are needed by individuals struggling to survive as a community that are different from those required by the individual attempting to survive alone in a hostile environment? Task: Create a "Survival Scrapbook" of articles and clippings about communal survival. Reflect upon the generalizations it may be possible to make about how groups successfully survive in crisis situations, and about when it is useful and logical for a group to "disturb the universe" in its efforts to survive.

     d.    *Language arts:* What are the traits of "survival literature?" What can be generalized about the relationship of plot, setting, characterization, conflict, and point of view in stories of survival? Tasks: Write and perform a skit in which characters from several of the novels find themselves thrown together in a difficult situation which requires each of them to use the skills and attributes that made them able to survive in their own novel. Engage in a forced debate about whether or not survivors and/or disturbers of the universe should be considered heroes. Shannon (1981) analyzes the ways in which child abuse has long been a part of folklore, a subject that students could investigate through library reseach.

     e.    *Health:* What is required for the body to survive? What aspects of an individual's health are within that individual's control? What aspects of the student's life need to be changed in order for him or her to better survive the stresses and demands of daily life? Task: Conduct or participate in a "Personal Health Fair," and create posters about lifestyle choices for a fuller, healthier life.

     f.    *Physical education:* What physical skills are required for wilderness survival? What is the relationship between attitude/mental health and physical skill/physical stamina in survival situations? Task: Develop an individualized training program related to survival skills, and chart progress over a specific period of time, setting goals and reflecting on effort required to achieve them.

     g.    *Art:* What professions are open to the artistically talented individual that provide enough income for survival? What are the truths behind the myth of the "starving artist?" Can and should society provide help to its artistically talented members? How does art contribute to the survival of a culture or society? Task: Investigate specific artists' lives, researching what they had to do to survive as artists and what aspects of their art has survived over time; if possible, interview a local artist as part of this investigation. Or, investigate the involvement of the U.S. government in the arts over time and take a stand on what the nature of its involvement should be today, especially given recent controversies regarding the health and status of the NEA.

h. *Music:* Why do some musical works survive over time and achieve the label of "classic"? What musical traditions of various historical periods have survived and are evident in the popular music of today? What musicians have "disturbed the universe" through their work? Task: Develop a time line of musical history presenting breakthroughs and changes in music theory, instrumentation, and definitions of music, noting how those elements are reflected in the work of contemporary rock, country, rap, jazz, and heavy metal composers and performers. Critique the work of a modern or contemporary composer who pushes the boundaries of popular notions of music (for instance, Frank Zappa, Karlheinz Stockhausen), reflecting on and predicting how their contributions to music will survive over time.

At the end of the poem "Faith Plotkin" in Mel Glenn's *Class Dismissed!* (1982), the adolescent female speaker, who has told the reader she skips school routinely and spends her time in the dark comfort of the theatre, says, "Can I please stay in the movies forever?" (83).

Faith's words echo the desire of so many middle school students who long for a respite from the turmoil of their lives. But comfortable as the coziness of movie world may be, most students know they cannot survive on popcorn alone. Eventually the movie ends, the lights come on, the concession stand closes, and the viewers have to exit the theatre and become actors in their own lives. Studying survival in a transdisciplinary unit context will help students begin to recognize both the difficulties inherent in any attempt to survive and/or disturb the universe regardless of the situation, and, hopefully, the necessity of taking charge of one's own destiny as individual and group member in order to do more than merely "survive."

# Works Cited

Glenn, Mel. 1982. *Class Dismissed!* New York: Clarion Books.

Kaywell, Joan F. 1993a. *Adolescents at Risk: A Guide to Fiction and Nonfiction for Young Adults, Parents, and Professionals.* Westport, CT: Greenwood Press.

————. 1993b. "Anne Frank's *The Diary of a Young Girl*: World War II and Young Adult Literature." In *Adolescent Literature as a Complement to the Classics,* edited by J. Kaywell, 13–36. Norwood, MA: Christopher Gordon.

Lindberg, Mary Anne. 1974. "Survival Literature in Children's Fiction." *Elementary English* 51(3): 329–35.

Lyman, F., C. Lopez, and A. Mindus. 1986. "Think-Links: The Shaping of Thought in Response to Reading." Unpublished manuscript. Columbia, MD.

McNair, Joseph. 1989. *Commander Coatrack Returns.* Boston: Houghton Mifflin.

Naylor, Phyllis Reynolds. 1981. *Footprints at the Window.* New York: Atheneum.

Paley, Nicholas. 1988. "Kids of Survival: Experiments in the Study of Literature." *English Journal* 77(5): 54–58.

Rosenberg, Adam. 1994. "Futurescape." *Instructor: The Middle Years* 103(6): 44–45.

Shannon, George. 1981. "The Survival of the Child: Abuse in Folklore." *Children's Literature in Education* 12(1): 34–38.

Silvey, Anita. "The Literature of Survival." 1986. *Horn Book Magazine* 62(3): 285.

Speare, Elizabeth George. 1988. "The Survival Story." *Horn Book Magazine* 64(2): 163–72.

*Snowbound.* 1977. Learning to Be Human Series. Learning Corporation of America (Distributed by Simon and Schuster). Videocassette.

Van Cleaf, David W. 1993. "Investigating Ghost Towns: Activities for Upper Elementary and Middle School Students." *Social Studies* 84(1): 37–41.

# Five

# The Delivery and Assessment of Transdisciplinary Instruction

I have always loved and wanted to emulate Ms. Finney, from Paula Danziger's *The Cat Ate My Gymsuit* (1974). Finney is an exemplary English teacher who acts on the assumptions that underlie this text. Marcy, the main character, notes that in Ms. Finney's classroom, "We worked hard, but it was fun" (32). There is a good deal of structure to Ms. Finney's class—on certain days during the week certain kinds of activities always take place, and students know they will study vocabulary, read books, respond to movies, and practice writing skills.

But Ms. Finney, unlike more traditional teachers, allows popcorn munching during movies. In her class, instead of writing book reports, students dress up as characters from the books they read, and then, in role, talk about their lives. When studying persuasion, students create television commercials to sell their books—another alternative to the book report. At one point, Finney has her students write a children's book, which they illustrate, bind, and deliver to youngsters in the local hospital. In place of a test over a list of literary terms, vocabulary, and spelling words, Finney's students participate in a board game. To teach the use of context clues, Ms. Finney becomes a detective who asks the students' help in figuring out a message on which coffee has been spilled. In Ms. Finney's classroom, students are constantly challenged to be responsible for their learning through the varied, well-designed motivational activities their teacher uses.

In my mind, Ms. Finney's assumption about the pedagogy best suited to the needs and interests of middle school students agrees with

87

those outlined in this text. Delivery of transdisciplinary curricular units should account for the fact that

> people make the difference—the caring, knowledgeable educators who—with intelligence and good humor—design an educational program based on a knowledge of the children whom they serve, tempered with flexibility and love. (Kerewsky 1988)

Ms. Finney certainly cares. The variety of instructional strategies she uses, designed to pique student interest and maintain their motivation, demonstrates her concern for them.

Teachers like Ms. Finney, who demonstrate a strong understanding of middle school students, will choose pedagogical strategies that are congruent with a desire for students to

make connections across content-area boundaries,

develop critical and creative thinking skills,

apply knowledge to real-life situations,

increase a sense of responsibility and respect for self and others,

develop a sense of community both within the school and beyond its doors,

identify their own talents,

appreciate the diversity of abilities others have to offer.

Like Ms. Finney, they know the importance of both structure and fun. Teachers of middle grade students will recognize the importance of planning instruction that moves from the concrete to the abstract and that allows for both socialization and independence. These teachers know the truth of the line from the Chinese proverb "I do and I understand" for all learners, but especially for middle school students, who are moving through so many rapid developmental changes.

Good middle school teachers also recognize that instructional methods used with students in the middle grades

> must be as varied as the students for whom they are designed. . . . Effective methods of grouping and instruction utilize the enthusiasm and energy that typify the age group. Active teaching and active learning, structured movement, project and group work, differentiated assignments which reflect student interests and abilities, hands-on activities, the use of educational technology, and other approaches that provide individual student participation, recognition, and accomplishment should be used in academic and other school-sponsored activities. Differentiation is vital to effective instruction for essential skills, higher level thinking, creativity, communication, affective outcomes, and exploratory activities. (Maryland Task Force on the Middle Years 1989, 40)

Because of the varied format for instruction and the constant involvement in hands-on projects, Marcy and her peers from *The Cat Ate My Gymsuit* will not forget the meaning of the term "understanding words in context." They will recognize the importance of having a real audience for a piece of writing, and they will feel comfortable taking risks thanks to their experiences in Ms. Finney's classroom.

Other specific teaching strategies that have proven effective with middle school students—because they are congruent with what we know about the developmental traits of young adolescents—include the many varieties of cooperative and/or collaborative learning, active teaching, inquiry strategies, and explicit teaching of thinking skills. All of these techniques must be supplemented by the use of learning materials that tap a variety of learning modes: laser disks, interactive video, computers, traditional print materials, videotapes, audio cassettes, and creative teacher-made materials.

When using literature as the basis for transdisciplinary planning, my first priority is to use strategies that allow students to connect with the world of the text. Thus, it seems to me, offering "bridges" or "purpose-for-reading" and motivational activities is crucial. Also, a multitext approach is more consistent with this middle school philosophy; for instance, Ms. Finney's book report alternative enables students who have read different texts to engage in discussion. Most importantly, middle school teachers who truly understand the middle school philosophy will embrace a reader-response approach to dealing with texts, and will use teaching strategies that allow individual students to interact with texts and to develop their language-processing skills within the context of all lessons.

Finally, the most effective middle school educators I know recognize the need to broaden the concept of assessment. They use portfolios, student self-evaluations, peer reports, and diverse kinds of student-generated products—even games, as Ms. Finney does—in addition to more traditional testing strategies so that all students have a chance to demonstrate not only their increased knowledge of factual material, but also their growth as readers and thinkers and partners in the learning process.

This chapter outlines several generic teaching and learning strategies and related assessment procedures that are philosophically congruent with transdisciplinary planning focused on works of literature. It also explains why these strategies are particularly suited to middle school students, and why they are especially appropriate for the kind of curricular organization advocated in this text. What I have attempted to do is to synthesize the theory and research discussed by thinkers and investigators from diverse fields. To mention all of those to whom I allude would be cumbersome; there is, however, a bibliography at the end of the chapter which details the sources upon which the chapter is based.

## The Benefits and Classroom Applications of Direct Instructional Models and Cooperative/ Collaborative Models for Middle School Students

### *Direct/Total Class Instruction*

By the time they reach middle school, most students have experienced a great deal of teacher-directed instruction. Therefore, I tried to provide for this kind of instruction in my own middle school classroom, and I urge my student teachers to do so, both because it makes a comfortable starting place for students potentially overwhelmed by the move to middle school, and because it does have its benefits. Brophy (1979) summarized the process of total class instruction and cited its benefits for teaching basic skills, especially to students who have not been all that successful as learners. In this model, the teacher presents information, assigns practice, and provides clear, specific, and immediate feedback.

> The teacher maintains an academic focus, keeping students involved in a lesson or engaged in seatwork, monitoring their performance, and providing individualized feedback. The pace is rapid in the sense that the class moves efficiently through the curriculum as a whole (and through the successive objectives of any given lesson), but progress from one objective to the next involves very small, easy steps. Success rates in answering teacher questions during lessons are high (about 75 percent), and success rates on assignments to be done independently are very high (approaching 100 percent). (Brophy 1979, 34)

Time on task in such classrooms is high and, according to Rosenshine and Stevens (1986), teachers assume responsibility for their students' learning.

Thus, when I use the direct instruction approach, *I* decide on the curricular goals, the objectives for the specific lesson, the materials to be used, and the organization of the learning environment. I begin with a review of previous lessons, then I collect homework and check it, make a twenty-minute presentation of new material, concepts, or skills during which student input is limited, and then conduct a question-and-answer session, using fairly low-level questions and a structured pattern for calling on students (to ensure a high success rate), followed by a short period of seatwork during which I circulate and provide corrective feedback.

With less successful students and those with an external locus of control, better results are achieved with lower-level questions, more repetition, and more structured support. Walberg (1990) notes that for highly motivated and successful students, the direct instruction model can be adapted by allowing more student initiation of teacher-student interaction, by asking more difficult questions with more rigorous probing, by assigning more complex homework, and by allowing for more student input into the lesson.

In the kinds of transdisciplinary units described in this book, direct instruction may be useful when a new skill is introduced, when the teacher wants to ensure basic comprehension of a difficult text, or when students lack confidence and so need to be weaned systemically from dependence on the teacher. Still, direct instruction is most useful when the goal is the teaching of basic skills. George and Alexander (1993) write,

> When creativity, problem solving, complex thinking, appreciation, or social and emotional education are the goals, the total class instruction process may not be the best method. It may even be that the direct instruction process is inimical to student growth in some areas other than basic skills, especially if students are older or more academically successful. Total class instruction may be inconsistent with the goals of social studies, humanities, the arts, and other essentially less cognitive and less factual areas. (152)

### Small-Group Instruction and Collaborative/Cooperative Strategies

One alternative to total class instruction is the use of small groups. Students arranged into groups of two to six for the purpose of working together to accomplish a task are involved in collaborative and/or cooperative learning. In these situations, I define my job as that of organizing and facilitating the learning process. Depending on the students' level of sophistication and skill in working together, I may do a great deal of orchestrating or may merely set the task and step out of the way. No matter what degree of involvement that I maintain, my objectives for the lesson in small-group work have as much to do with the affective domain as with the cognitive.

"Collaborative" strategies are those that involve students in clarifying existing knowledge and constructing new knowledge together through talk. Cooperative strategies almost always involve collaboration, but they require a more structured organization; students work as teams toward a common objective and team rewards while demonstrating individual accountability within the team structure. I often choose collaborative strategies to use in my university classroom because of my commitment to the development of speaking and listening skills and my knowledge of the power of speaking as a learning tool. In general, when teachers choose true cooperative strategies, they demonstrate a commitment to the systematic development of the social skills needed for cooperative endeavors.

Collaborative activities include informal partner work for homework review or peer editing of first drafts of writing, as well as various kinds of small-group activities; any time students talk and listen as a way to clarify and extend their knowledge and understanding, they are collaborating. I often use collaborative activities to help activate the students' cognitive structure at the beginning of class sessions. For example, students might be told to "think/pair/share"; that is, they may brainstorm individually about the list of items they would pack if told they were going into hiding for an indefinite period of time and had an hour to get ready as an introduction to Anne Frank's *The Diary of a Young Girl* (1952). After a given amount of time, they share their list with a partner, making any changes in their own list as a result of this brief discussion. Then, discussion in a large-group setting occurs, and I feel at least somewhat assured that everyone in the class has had an opportunity to consider the issue and to gather their thoughts on it.

At other times, I use collaborative strategies as a way to maintain high levels of student involvement during a class session, allowing students to process information and apply it as they talk with one another. For example, after reading silently during a directed reading activity, students might be asked to check their answers to the "purpose-for-reading" questions with a small group of their peers. As a way to begin a discussion about a reading assignment, I sometimes ask students to generate with their peers a list of questions they hope the text will answer.

Middle school students are social creatures who value time to talk with their friends. Collaborative strategies allow teachers to tap this interest in socializing and to use it constructively.

There are any number of ways to group students for collaborative activities. Sometimes it is useful to have students with similar levels of reading skill work together to make sense of whatever text they may have been reading. Sometimes students who share a similar skill deficiency can work together on an activity designed to reinforce that skill; thus, one group of students having trouble punctuating dialogue may be working together to peer edit for that skill, while another group of students may be focusing their peer-editing efforts on sentence variety.

Students may be grouped according to interest in a project, or they may be allowed to choose their own groups according to their desire to socialize. Sometimes, teachers may decide to group unlikely students together in an effort to foster tolerance and social acceptance, while at other times, for tutorial reasons, the teacher may decide to pair a student who needs special help because of a lack of competence with a student who has skill in the same area. Sometimes, students can be grouped most effectively based on learning-style preference; for instance, if groups of students have to create a product of some sort that synthesizes a novel they have read, the visual learners may be grouped together to generate a poster or chart, while the kinesthetic learners might be grouped together to perform a skit. At times teachers will determine group membership based on personality so as to avoid conflicts and increase group productivity. In my Young Adult Literature class, I sometimes will put all the talkative students with strong personalities together; they have to learn to listen and take turns in order to accomplish their given task. Meanwhile, the group of students who are quieter and less likely to volunteer their answers in a large group has a forum in which to talk without being overshadowed by their more vocal peers. I find it interesting to watch how leaders emerge from among these quieter students when they have the opportunity to use those talents.

It is true that students who have had little opportunity to work in groups frequently fail to demonstrate the self-control and self-monitoring skill needed to accomplish tasks in groups. If this is the case, the teacher will choose to have students work only as partners on very focused, well-defined tasks until they begin to demonstrate the social skills needed to move into larger groupings. But in all collaborative activities, the objective is for students to extend their individual knowledge or skill through working with others.

Researchers who discuss the benefits of cooperative learning strategies have long recognized the need to *teach* students the social skills necessary for true cooperation. If students are merely thrown together and assigned a task, they may fail. Interactive classrooms probably demand more teacher sensitivity to students' situations than other classroom environments. In a classroom that is teacher-directed and filled with teacher talk, students only have to endure what may be poor instruction. However, if teachers fail to help students acquire the skills needed for success in cooperative endeavors, and then set them tasks requiring those skills, they are asking students to participate in a poor instructional environment, which seems potentially even more damaging to their educational progress.

True cooperative learning strategies involve several key components: a common goal toward which a group of students is working; individual accountability; and opportunities for each student to succeed. As an example, Slavin (1980, 1990) describes the process of organizing students into teams, assigning them material to study (how to change from Fahrenheit to centigrade or how to do metric conversions), assessing individual learning through traditional quizzes or game situations, and then recognizing the entire team once each member has demonstrated accomplishment of the skill.

Adults constantly find themselves in situations involving these components. Drivers on the beltway in the morning share the goal of safe arrival at their destination. Individually, they have to know and act on the rules of the road, adapting to difficult weather conditions or overcoming technical problems that may arise in their vehicles. If everyone does his or her "job" correctly, rush hour goes smoothly, and there are no tie-ups; everyone is rewarded. Students who never have the opportunity to learn the give and take of cooperation are likely to grow up without having had to overcome the kind of egotism which can lead to accidents on the road, as well as to lack of communication in a marriage, or failure to be good team players on the job.

Here is an overview of several well-known strategies, as applied in literature-based transdisciplinary units, which, when used appropriately, involve the key components of cooperative learning and lead to significant benefits. Cooperative learning strategies increase motivation, improve positive relationships with peers—including students often otherwise perceived as "different"—and stimulate higher-level thinking/problem-solving skills.

**Teams/Games/Tournaments.** This is a useful learning strategy, especially for factual material, such as definitions of terms, problem-solving processes and rules/principles. In Chapter 2, "There's No Place Like Home," one of the unit goals is "Students will be able to research the concept of 'home' from a variety of perspectives." Thus, for example, in adapting the perspective of health professionals, students might have to learn a definition for "stress," identify "good" and "bad" stress, list kinds of stressors, and describe the elements in an individual's home situation that can cause stress, using examples from their literary experiences to support their work.

In teams of four or five, students study this information—they may have library time to find it, they may hear a lecture from a social worker on it, they may read about stress in a textbook or in other resources. Students know their teams will compete after a specified amount of time in a game or tournament that will require this knowledge base. Individual rewards or grades will be given based on the *team* performance in this game or tournament. Thus, according to Slavin (1984), students will want to help their peers master the information and will work as a team in the review process. Slavin also describes the variation on this strategy he calls "Student Teams Achievement Divisions," in which individual mastery is assessed through small quizzes.

**Round-Robin and Inside-Outside Circle.** Both Round-Robin and Inside-Outside Circle are useful in review situations. In Round-Robin, students are assigned to small groups. Each individual shares—verbally or in writing—something he or she has learned about a given topic. The act of hearing what a peer has noted to be of importance helps trigger the memories of other group members; together, the group constructs a collaborative overview of the topic through collective association. In Inside-Outside Circle, students stand in concentric circles facing a partner. The inside circle faces the outside; the outside circle faces the inside. The teacher calls out review questions. First the inside circle might have to answer while the partner in the outer circle checks that answer. The circles then rotate so that for each question, students work with a different partner.

Imagine students have the "Conflict and Confrontation" unit from Chapter 3. In this unit, each student has read *Gulf* (Westall 1992) and at least two other titles of his or her own choice. To help students recognize how much they have learned about the ways in which conflict is essential to plot in a piece of literature, the teacher might first use Round-Robin, asking students in groups to create charts of concepts about conflict in literature. One student might write "One kind of conflict is person versus environment." The paper is passed to the next group member who adds, "Another is person versus self." Someone adds that conflict can arise over the interpretation of a piece of literature. Someone then might add that the characters often reflect different kinds of responses to the same situation in a text, and that readers who identify with different characters may then find themselves in conflict.

Switching to Inside-Outside Circle, I would then ask questions that force students to apply their knowledge of conflict. "Give an example from *Gulf* of . . ." or "Give an example from one of your independently read texts of . . ." or "Give an example of how conflict is inherent in the natural world" or "Here's a situation involving conflict. How would you resolve it?" There is not one right answer to any of these questions; the partners should be able to engage in some dialogue as one partner offers a response and the other one reacts to what they offer.

**Jigsaw and Variations.** The "Surviving, Living, and Disturbing the Universe" unit described in Chapter 4 is organized on the principles of the jigsaw. In general, the material to be studied is divided into a specific number of segments; in the "Survival" unit, there are seven groups of three titles each. Next, students are assigned to teams of the same number of participants as there are segments of material; thus, students eventually work in groups of seven. Four students might read the same three titles (one from each survival genre). In "expert" groups they check each other's understanding of those titles, making sure they have followed the plot, know the relationships among the characters, understand the tensions and themes, and so forth. Then, they are reassigned to larger groups of seven students, each of whom has read a different title from each of the three categories. As experts on their own titles, students work together to generalize about the books using the teacher's guidelines. It is probably easier to envision the jigsaw procedure using a chart format:

## Text Sets

| Physical Survival | Survival in Emotional Crisis | Disturbing the Universe |
|---|---|---|
| 1. *The Goats*<br><br>Students a,b,c,d | *Staying Fat for Sarah Byrnes* | *Song of Be* |
| 2. *Downriver*<br><br>Students e,f,g,h | *Abby, My Love* | *Don't Care High* |
| 3. *All But My Life*<br><br>Students i,j,k,l | *Dean Duffy* | *White Lilacs* |

4-7 (One title from each category with 4 different students per group.)

At first, students a, b, c, and d work together to become "experts" on the titles they have read in common. Their first title, on physical survival, will be *The Goats* (Cole 1987); eventually they will work together to process both *Staying Fat for Sarah Byrnes* (Crutcher 1993) and *Song of Be* (Beake 1993). After they feel comfortable with each title, they regroup. Now, students a, e, and i, students b, f, and j, students c, g, and k, and students d, h, and l will work together to find similarities and differences among the three books on physical survival. In this group, there will be an "expert" on *The Goats, Downriver* (Hobbs 1991), *All but My Life* (Klein 1957), and each of the other titles about physical survival.

The individual accountability factor comes into play in the jigsaw strategy as students serve as "experts." They then have to work as a group to accomplish a task that requires their cooperation; in the case of the "Survival" unit, questions are outlined that require synthesis on the part of the group members after they have shared their "expert" knowledge. The "group investigator" strategy is similar to the jigsaw technique in that each individual within a team is responsible for researching one aspect of a topic. After sharing their findings, individuals have to collaborate to produce a group report, which is presented in some format to the class as a whole.

One final caution about using cooperative strategies: Teachers who want to use collaborative/cooperative strategies need to plan effectively before implementing them in their classrooms. I try to take into consideration several important elements of the lesson before assigning students cooperative tasks:

Make certain the topic lends itself to real discussion.

Provide focusing questions.

Ensure the room arrangement facilitates interaction by arranging circles of chairs, tables at which several students can sit, and desks moved into larger groups (all of which allow for conversation better than desks arranged in rows).

Help students play various roles—chair, recorder, reporter, facilitator, time keeper, evaluator—within cooperative groups.

Maintain control over group constituency.

Provide clear directions and set expectations.

Monitor group progress and provide feedback and evaluation (Figure 5–1). Include opportunities for students to engage in both self- and peer-evaluation of their participation and of the group process (Stover, Neubert, and Lawlor 1993, 55–56).

## Figure 5–1
### Five Types of Rating Checklists

---

## FIVE TYPES OF RATING CHECKLISTS
(Source Unknown)

A rating sheet, based upon the objectives previously agreed upon, often helps each group diagnose its own difficulties and evaluate its own accomplishments. The same holds true for the individual. The first two forms may be used with beginners.

GROUP'S SELF-RATING
Purpose:_____

1. Did we get to work promptly?
2. Did we stick to the point?

3. Did we work quietly?

4. Did all contribute?
5. Did we ask for help as soon as we needed it?
6. What did we accomplish?_____

Such a reaction sheet, completed by the group, serves as impetus for a class evaluation that reemphasizes the purpose of the experience and the means used for its accomplishment.

BEGINNER'S CHECKLIST FOR SELF-RATING
Subject:_____

1. Did I prepare sufficiently?

2. Did I follow directions?

3. Did I make the best use of my time?

4. Did I work without disturbing other groups?
5. My chief contribution to the group was:_____

After several meetings, let students draw names to rate one other member.

EVALUATION OF A GROUP MEMBER
1. What was his or her chief contribution?
2. What factor should he or she first try to improve?
3. Evaluation by:_____

With an experienced group, a more complete rating is possible. In developing a form, select only times in which instruction has been given and ask the student to select several aspects of his or her performance to evaluate in a brief essay.

CHECKLIST FOR SELF-RATING BY MORE MATURE STUDENTS
1. Did I assume the responsibility the group wished?
2. Did I listen alertly?
3. Did I willingly express my own point of view?
4. Did I try to understand the viewpoint of others?
5. Did I attempt to assess the strengths and weaknesses of all opinions expressed?
6. Did I encourage those who seemed reluctant to speak?
7. Did I help the chairperson maintain a friendly, businesslike atmosphere?

8. Did I keep the discussion moving purposefully?
9. Did I subordinate my own wishes to further the aim of the group?
10. My greatest contribution to the group was:_____

CHECKLIST FOR RATING GROUP MEMBERS
After the importance of group solidarity has become an accepted tenet of the thinking of the majority, it is often beneficial to have students rate all members. The following form has been used for that purpose. It is more appropriate for groups keeping the same personnel for several meetings.

Number the names of members alphabetically:

| | |
|---|---|
| 1. Adams, Ruth | 4. Jones, Ann Marie |
| 2. Bell, Richard | 5. Lee, Edward |
| 3. Harris, John | 6. Swenson, Sondra |

Use the corresponding number for the checklist. Rate from 1 (excellent) to 5 (poor).

GROUP MEMBERS

| | 1 | 2 | 3 | 4 |
|---|---|---|---|---|
| 1. Carries out responsibilities | 5 | | | |
| 2. Cooperates in discussion | 1 | | | |
| 3. Expresses self clearly | 1 | | | |
| 4. Considers all viewpoints | 2 | | | |
| 5. Encourages others | 2 | | | |
| 6. Shows interest in group's success | 5 | | | |

Focusing on the evaluation can, of course, be overdone. It is useful, at first, as a teaching device to emphasize standards. When students become more adept at group work, it may only be needed rarely.

# Motivation and the Transdisciplinary Curriculum

## *Motivation Theory*

Marcy Lewis from *The Cat Ate My Gymsuit* is motivated to learn in Ms. Finney's classroom because her time with Ms. Finney is both fun and constructive. Ms. Finney instinctively applies the principles of motivation theory articulated by various researchers.

First of all, it is difficult for a learner to concentrate on intellectual endeavors if survival needs, such as food, water, and shelter, are not met. Additionally, students who feel either physically or emotionally unsafe in the environment are not always at their best academically. Exemplary middle schools provide advisory sessions during which students work with an adult on a regular basis to deal with the anxieties of adolescence, to solve conflicts, and to process their experiences both in and out of school. Also, exemplary middle school teachers recognize students' needs for belonging and self-esteem, and so avoid ridicule, sarcasm, and other strategies that demean and belittle, while employing strategies that provide students opportunities to feel a part of a larger whole and to feel individually successful (Wiles and Bondi 1993; George and Alexander 1993). In classrooms in which transdisciplinary units based on young adult literature unfold, students' individual responses to texts, no matter how different from the teacher's own interpretation, need to be accepted and used as the starting point for discussion and learning.

Good middle school teachers know the difference between students who feel themselves to be pawns and those who feel themselves to be originators in life, between those students who attribute success or failure to external forces and those who can accept responsibility appropriately for what happens to them. Such teachers want all their students to perceive themselves as able to take responsibility for their actions, for their learning, and for their corner of the world. Therefore, it seems to me, we *have* to allow students some choice over their reading selections and some input into the direction of study based upon those texts.

In *Alice the Brave* (1995) by Phyllis Reynolds Naylor, the most important lesson Alice learns during the eventful summer prior to eighth grade is that *she* can decide whether to be fearful or to conquer her fears. She spends much of July and August living in terror that her peers will discover that not only is she unable to swim in deep water, but that she is frightened to death by the mere prospect. The worst finally happens; a group of boys picks her up, intending to dunk her into the pool, but they back off when she becomes hysterical. Until Alice takes charge of her situation, she cannot enjoy the summer activities, keeps herself distant from her friends, and seems constantly on edge at home because of her fears.

Fortunately, her older brother, Lester, normally perceived by Alice to be a pain, comes to her rescue. With infinite patience, he teaches her what she needs to know, breaking down her fears a step at a time until she finally asks him to throw her into the deep end of the pool. Alice says, after this lesson, ". . . now I was learning to trust myself. . . . This was about the best day of my life. I was so afraid before, and suddenly I can wake up in the mornings and not have to worry anymore" (105). Later, she remarks that the summer was important to her because she had learned that

if any of the other hundred and one awful possibilities that lurked around the corner *were* to happen, I could take it. It might knock me down temporarily, but it wouldn't put me out. Because I had guts. . . . Alice the brave, that was me. (124)

Like Alice, Marcy Lewis has to overcome her perception of herself as an overweight girl not worthy of attention from teachers, her parents, and boys. Ms. Finney's teaching strategies and her belief in Marcy all contribute, in the end, to Marcy's willingness to take a public stand against both her principal and her father when Ms. Finney is fired. Good middle school teachers recognize how *their* beliefs about students' personal competence affect students' perceptions of their own abilities to take control of their lives. Helping students accept responsibility for studying; for setting realistic goals and accomplishing them step-by-step; and in general, for taking charge of their lives instead of allowing themselves to be the victims of circumstance are key attributes of the successful middle school teacher.

There are several generic components of motivation that middle school teachers should understand, especially when they are attempting to invite students to become partners in transdisciplinary inquiry. One component of highly motivating learning situations is that they provide students with opportunities to be successful. Thus teachers need to know their students and their students' capabilities so that lessons build on what students already know and can do. When Lester teaches Alice to swim better, he starts by having her dog-paddle as far as she can across the pool at the shallow end, and praises her for having learned that much on her own. He stays beside her in the water as she gradually moves into water of increasing depth. He holds her hand as she jumps off the side into water that is first three feet deep, then four feet, then five, six, and so on. At the deep end, he asks her to swim just one stroke from the side toward his outstretched hand. He gradually backs away from her, and praises her for each successive effort. Eventually, *she* decides she is ready for the ultimate test of her newly acquired skill; she asks him to try tossing her out into the water, and then *she* decides to use the board. Had Lester started out by trying to coax Alice into deep water, bemoaning her lack of confidence, and telling her "It's easy!" or "Try harder!," Alice probably would have given up on the lesson.

Rosenbery, et al. (1992) provide an example of the importance of structuring for success in a school setting. They describe a project in which teachers helped nonnative English-speaking students, who had very little experience "doing science," with the scientific method. At the beginning of the school year, these students overgeneralized from personal experiences and failed to use logical reasoning when engaged in problem solving. By collaborating with the students, modeling the strategies of successful scientists, and building on small successes, teachers found that the students had learned to reason better by the end of the school year. They were more able to hypothesize and to engage in experimentation in a structured way in order to evaluate those hypotheses.

Another component of the motivating learning situation is that students are provided with knowledge of the results of their efforts. As a child, I wanted desperately to be a part of a sports team, but I was not naturally athletic and lacked both grace and coordination. I recall with great frustration my encounters with P.E. teachers who shouted, "Keep your eye on the ball!" during the softball unit or "Defend the basket" during the basketball unit. I had my eye on the ball. That was my problem; I could see it coming right at me, and was scared to death of it! I had no idea *how* to defend the basket. I needed specific feedback about what I was doing wrong and what I should be doing instead. Where should my hands have gone in relationship to the other player and my own body when I was attempting to defend the basket?

The teacher who merely writes on a student's paper, "Awkward!" succumbs to the same mistake. The student needs to know *why* the wording is awkward, needs to have a sense of other possible options, and needs to learn strategies for determining independently whether or not a sentence reads awkwardly. Similarly, students need to know the specific reasons for success. What did the batter do *this* time that resulted in a hit instead of a strikeout? Why is *this* sentence well phrased and successful in communicating to its audience?

Teachers also need to grab the attention of their middle school students who have much else on their minds and much else to worry about besides school. A variety of instructional strategies and materials helps keep students on their toes. Varying vocal inflections, modeling a personal willingness to deviate from set expectations by taking on a role, or even just experimenting with the format of the classroom environment do the same. The teacher who dresses up as Pythagoras (complete with toga and crown of laurel leafs) on the day he introduces the Pythagorean theorem and describes how he discovered it and what it means, will definitely catch his students' attention. The teacher who brings in her great-grandfather's Civil War sword or the contract, signed by her aunt as a first-year teacher in the early part of this century, that prohibited her from walking in public with a man is more likely to make an historical period come alive as a bridge into a book like Hunt's *Across Five Aprils* or *His Banner Over Me* by Little than is the teacher who merely says, "Read Chapter 1 for tomorrow." Kim and Kellough (1995) provide a list of over two hundred general and discipline-based motivational strategies teachers can use to generate interest in their lessons, ranging from the traditional use of audio-visual materials to more creative techniques, such as devising variations on game shows or having students use newer technologies—such as hyper-cards and laser disks—through which to present what they have learned (599–611).

Students seem to learn best from teachers who demonstrate that they respect their students and care about them as people; that they are not just names on the class roster. In short, students learn best from teachers who create warm, caring environments. My department chair at the junior high school where I taught used to tell us, "If you're with them at the basketball game, or dance, or lock-in Friday night, they'll be with you in class Monday morning." Teachers who make the effort to know which student had a difficult game, who placed in the Forensics meet, who did a good job in the chorus of the spring play, or who did well on a science test are letting students know they recognize their individuality. The good middle school teacher knows instinctively when to compliment a girl with a new haircut—and when to say nothing because it is clear she is not pleased with the result. The advisory practice employed in many middle schools—a time built into the daily schedule during which students work with an adult to deal with the anxieties, conflicts, and experiences of adolescence (often the adult stays with the same group of students from the time they enter middle school until they leave)—provides opportunities for adults and adolescents to work together as people outside their roles as teachers and students. The transdisciplinary structures based on literature about the adolescent experience that are described in this text: allow students to build on their individual strengths; tap students' interests; and provide a chance for students to feel responsibility for their education—all components of a thriving classroom environment in which students feel valued.

Anything the teacher can do to reduce anxiety will also help students' motivation to learn. For some students, a bit of anxiety can be positive; their adrenaline starts to flow, and their senses are sharpened. But for many middle school students anxiety induces mental and emotional paralysis—which is not conducive to learning. I can recall quite vividly, for example, getting a social studies test in seventh grade and realizing very quickly I could not answer the first question. I went on to number 2. When I could not answer it, my hands began to sweat. I tried number 3; again, I did not know the correct response. My stomach began to ache. By the time I got to number 4, I could barely read the question because panic had set in; the rest of the test was a nightmare.

Fortunately for me, that test was one of the very few I recall as having been problematic. Many students, however, who have that same kind of experience over and over again begin to feel failure is inevitable. The special education teacher in Jamie Gilson's *Do Bananas Chew Gum?* (1980) spends a long time with the main character, engaging him in activities designed to show him just how good a thinker he is in spite of his reading difficulties. He has to develop some confidence in his abilities before he can begin learning; because he has trouble reading, the teacher provides him with strategies to help him cope when reading is required.

In general, middle school teachers need to help their students know what to expect—before taking a test, when working on a group project, or a difficult book that stretches their reading level somewhat. They need help breaking down large projects into manageable steps; as they accomplish each task, they feel a level of success that allows them to have the confidence to move on. Thus, starting the year by saying to the students, "Now, what would you like to do this year?" when they have never been a part of the planning process before is likely to overwhelm them. They need help recognizing what they know and what they do not know and how they can close the gaps that exist in their knowledge and skills base, and they need to know the teacher will provide a safety net while they practice these skills until, like Alice, they are willing to perform without it. A final component of the motivational learning situation is the judicious use of reinforcement by the teacher.

Middle school students who tend to be concrete in their thinking and egocentric in their perceptions frequently respond well to rewards and reinforcement. The tricky part of using rewards, however, is that what students perceive as a reward may never occur to the teacher to offer. Thus, teachers need to talk to their students about what motivates them, what acts as a true incentive and a true reward. Middle school students—highly social creatures who are rushed from class to class and given four minutes to run from the gym on one side of the school to the science lab on the other and maybe ten minutes to eat lunch once they have gone to their locker, used the restroom, and stood in line in the cafeteria—often want, more than anything, five minutes to themselves to talk with their friends. They might want to be assured of getting to the lunchroom first. They might want to have a radio or tape playing during writing/reading time. They may want a pizza party, a homework pass, a chance to have a discussion outside under a tree.

Some students have internalized the motivation to learn, and they just want to be left alone to do the reading or the research or the project, knowing that learning can be its own reward; other students, especially those with less-than-glowing academic track records, need teachers who can help by validating and reinforcing their efforts. They need to know that their successes, however small, will be honored.

The teacher who notes +4/10 and comments, "Your answer to number three is right on target" sends a very different message than the one who simply writes –6/10 = F.

### *"Bridging"—Motivating Students to Read and Learn*

In a 1966 *English Journal* article titled "Listen My Children and You Shall Read," Edmund Farrell wrote,

> If I were asked what the most serious shortcoming is of the student teachers I observe, I would reply, "Their failure to motivate interest in a selection, to build bridges between students' concerns and experiences and the experiences recorded in the literature." Student teachers don't realize that assigning a selection and teaching it are not synonymous.
> I can't tell any teacher, student or otherwise, what bridges to build, for what he constructs depends upon what he knows about himself, his students, and his material. (44)

Every so often, one of my student teachers will complain about the seeming lack of motivation to learn that his or her students are exhibiting. Upon analysis, it becomes clear that the student teacher has failed to help the students see the connections between the world of the classroom and the world outside the classroom—that middle school students, still very concrete thinkers, need to see. But the student teacher might protest that forcing students to be interested in the material is not her job. She might say students should have internal motivation to learn, stating that students will never grow to love learning if they are "bribed" into it. The use of bridges, of tying the content or skill to be learned to some aspect of the students' lives and experiences, is a way to help students move away from reliance on extrinsic rewards.

Many years ago I watched a gifted student teacher use a "bridge" in her American literature class that exemplifies Farrell's position. Her students arrived after lunch for her class, typically entering the room, depositing their materials on "their" desks, and then going back out into the hall to socialize until the bell rang. On this particular day, she systematically moved the students' belongings to other desks, and then rearranged the desks so that they touched each other in groups of three and four. When students reentered the classroom, they looked at the new arrangements, and, frowning but without much conversation, replaced the books in their original locations and separated the desks. The drill for the day, posted on the board, directed, "Freewrite about what was different about the room when you entered it for class and why you reacted as you did to the changes you observed." After a brief writing period, the teacher asked students to talk about what they had written. They commented on their need for personal space, on their need for structure, on their lack of comfort sitting too close to other students not of their own choosing, on their lack of comfort knowing that someone had touched their belongings. Then, the teacher gave them copies of Frost's poem "Mending Wall" (1939), instructing them to listen as she read it for ways in which the characters' positions were similar and different from those they had just expressed. This activity, which took maybe five minutes to do, allowed the students the perfect "in" to a poem with the repeated line, "good fences make good neighbors."

A bridge can merely be a question, such as "What are some adjectives you associate with spring?", prior to reading e. e. cummings' piece "in Just —." It can be a simple activity, such as the one described above. It can involve writing, speaking, listening, or reading; prior to a lesson on the French Revolution, a teacher might have students read a newspaper article about recent upheavals in Bosnia or Serbia and then ask students to describe the relationships involved in the conflicts there. Students might be asked to think creatively—for instance, they might have to work in groups to brainstorm a list of characteristics of the ideal city. Then, as a unit on "The City" unfolds, they use this list as a touchstone, adding to it, and crossing off items as they learn more and more about the nature of cities.

The teacher might structure a fairly elaborate activity in order to provide students with a concrete experience upon which discussion of abstract concepts will build. For example, Olzewski and Montenaro (1995), introducing a unit on multicultural interdependence, hand their students index cards containing the name of a country and categories of information to be filled in through library research efforts. One student may have France, another Kuwait, another Brazil. Each student has to find out the national language, major religions, major exports and imports, ties to other countries (as through colonization or trade), current ruler, current state of suffrage, party system, date of independence, and major agricultural products.

After students have completed their research (if the teacher wants to save time, he or she can distribute completed cards), the teacher throws a ball of yarn to someone. That student has to describe her country and throw the ball to someone else. After the students are entwined in a web of string, the teacher starts to ask questions, such as "How many countries would be affected by a sudden drop in the price of oil?" or "Who would be affected by a coup in [X country]?" Students sit down if their country would be touched by events taking place elsewhere around the world. Then, the teacher asks them to generalize about what this activity has shown them. In a very graphic, tangible way, they are able to recognize the interdependence of the countries of the world—a useful bridge into any number of units, including those centered on concepts like conflict, dependence, or survival.

Sometimes bridges in the natural world are simple constructions; a rope or a log may suffice to allow the traveler to move from point *a* to point *b* over some obstacle. Other times, the bridge has to be much more elaborate, as is the case with the Chesapeake Bay Bridge-Tunnel or the Golden Gate Bridge. Teachers need to know how complex a bridge their students will need prior to beginning a unit or a lesson. I find that asking students to talk about which one tool out of a list of ten they would find most useful were they to be stranded in the Canadian wilderness—the situation in which the main character finds himself in *Hatchet* (1987) by Paulsen—suffices as an introduction to that book; after we have our discussion, my students are eager to read.

However, students may need a great deal of information before they are able to enter into the world of a text. Thus, an entire unit on the ecosystems, developed by the teachers and presented in the traditional curriculum format of lessons that build upon each other sequentially might become the "bridge" into a unit on "environments" designed with student input and centered on their questions and concerns. Until students know something about an historical event such as the Holocaust or about the current state of affairs in Bosnia, Croatia, and Yugoslavia, they may have little interest in reading either *The Diary of a Young Girl* (Frank 1952) or *Zlata's Diary* (Filipovic 1994). As one young man responded when handed *Zlata's Diary* without a motivator, knowing he was to read a certain number of pages by the next day, "I don't wanna read some dumb ol' diary, specially not one by some girl from some foreign country."

On the other hand, the students of Sykesville Middle School in rural Maryland who had Rita Karr (Stover with Karr 1990) *were* motivated to read *Shadows Across the Sun* (1983), a novel set in the former Soviet Union by Russian young-adult author Likhanov because Karr asked them, before even telling them about the book, to write the letter they would write to their best friend upon learning that they were to be relocated to Moscow for an indefinite period of time. They talked about these letters and generalized about their conceptions of that city, identifying what they were "certain" were truthful statements about life there, and what questions they had. They read the novel and got involved with Fedya and Lena, characters who touched their hearts because they were embarrassed by their parents, were anxious about their developing interest in each other, and were concerned about school tasks, friendships, and their futures. Because of their sense of connection with these characters, the *students* then asked if they could do research on Moscow and the Soviet Union's history. They wanted to keep scrapbooks of newspaper articles about that region of the world and analyze the biases they perceived in its presentation. They wanted to read more books about "kids growing up" there—and about adolescents growing up in other countries.

In Karr's classroom, the study of the novel was the "bridge" that transported students into transdisciplinary inquiry based on their interest and a desire to learn. When her students met students at the Russian Embassy School in Washington, D.C., and compared notes about cute boys/girls, homework, teachers who were too strict, favorite TV shows, and music, Karr knew her eighth graders' experiences with the text had changed their lives (Stover with Karr 1990).

### Integrating Language-Processing and Thinking Skills Throughout the Curriculum

All of the bridges described in the previous section involved students in connecting their lived experience with the content to be studied. Additionally, they required students to use all the language (reading, writing, speaking, listening) and thinking skills required for successful completion of almost any task in life. The teaching of content and skills in an integrated manner is an essential component of transdisciplinary planning centered on young adult literature.

Because texts form the heart of this curriculum students have to use their existing reading skills and practice new ones for every concept they investigate. Because it is possible to find diverse kinds of texts—mysteries, poetry, biographies, novels, essays—about almost any concept, students will be able to practice reading for different purposes. Because they will frequently have to become the "expert" on a given text, taking responsibility for presenting it to others, they will have to practice summarization skills: they will have to determine what is most important in a text and share that with others, using details to support their point of view. Because they will often work in groups to synthesize their individual experiences about a concept with gathered information representing diverse perspectives, they will have to practice generalizing skills.

As students share their responses to texts, they practice speaking and listening skills. As they gather information and study a concept from multiple perspectives, they should have opportunities to practice listening and speaking for various purposes. They will be unable to form generalizations or to generate hypotheses and conclusions that account for all available data unless they listen to each other share various pieces of information. For example, in the "Conflict and Confrontation" unit described in Chapter 3, one of the suggested tasks is for students to become the ambassador from a country considered a "hot spot" and to present a request for a specific kind of U.S. involvement/noninvolvement to someone playing the role of the president of the United States. To be successful, students will have to use formal levels of diction, organizational skills, persuasion, and supporting documentation. The "president" will have to listen critically in order to raise questions, probe for the weaknesses in the presenter's argument, and ultimately, determine whether the proposed course of action is viable for the United States.

Another suggested task is for students to listen to various musical compositions representing different periods in history and to describe them in terms of conflict and conflict resolution. They will have to attend to various aspects of the composition, practicing critical analysis of the piece—skills similar to those involved in the "hot spot" exercise, but applied in a very different context.

To complete the proposed task that draws on scientific knowledge and principles, that of creating a videotape describing conflict in the natural world, students will have to determine who their desired audience will be and speak accordingly; if they choose to create a video for younger students, for instance, they will have to use language and organizational structures quite different from those they use when engaged in the "hot spot" activity.

Writing, both as a tool to enhance learning and as a tool to demonstrate learning, permeates the literature-based transdisciplinary curriculum. Students write to keep track of their responses to texts, to keep track of information gathered from various sources, and to keep track of progress in small groups. They write to discover what they already know, to process what they are learning, and to organize what they have learned. They write individually, and they write collaboratively. They write about their observations of the natural world, they write to sort out their feelings, they write to express their opinions. They write to generalize, to indicate comprehension, to find errors in their thinking, to personalize information. Their writing provides them—and their teachers—with a record of their thoughts over time, so they can assess their progress and set new goals.

Consider the "Conflict and Confrontation" unit. One of the unit-initiating activities—"cubing"—described in Chapter 3 is an example of how writing can stimulate the writer to explore multiple perspectives on a topic. The webbing activity, also a sample bridge for the unit, involves students collaboratively in tapping prior associations and experiences with conflict so that they have a starting point from which to raise questions that can then guide their reading and course of study. Providing "purpose-for-reading" questions for students to answer while they read the various texts provides a database they can later use to make generalizations about the relationship between conflict and plot development.

The suggested unit tasks described in earlier chapters provide opportunities for students to experiment with various genres and to write for various purposes to various audiences. Writing a fictionalized or autobiographical account of conflict leading to personal growth involves different skills than, with a group, writing a set of procedures for resolving conflict or, individually, creating a personal plan for reducing stress, which in turn requires a different set of skills from writing captions for a scrapbook of articles demonstrating the use of math to deal with daily conflict.

We have known for almost twenty years that writing aids thinking and learning because it requires a degree of commitment—to words, sentence structure, and overall organization—not necessary in speech. Writers engage simultaneously in various modes of learning. They see, feel, and think about what they are saying on paper all at once. In general, writing helps students gain authority and independence as learners. Many researchers find that writing acts as a powerful heuristic and aid to thinking, although recent research such as that conducted by Sudol and Sudol (1995), and Labbo, Hoffman, and Rosen (1995), indicates that teachers do have to use writing as a learning tool carefully, or they can unintentionally make the writing process more difficult.

In order to make connections across traditional disciplinary boundaries, whether listening, speaking, reading, or writing, students have to be active as thinkers. They have to organize information, clarify it, interpret it, and reflect on the implications of their observations and generalizations. For example, after reading several texts about survival in different kinds of circumstances (see Chapter 4), students might be directed to write a paper in which they argue that $X$ is an essential quality of the survivor. For each character whom they perceive to have the quality, Jackie Sachs, a teacher at Magothy River Middle School, in Anne Arundel County, Maryland, asks students to complete a chart (see Figure 5–2). To do so, students have to make a generalization, which means they have to interpret the texts they read based on a developing database about the characters in those texts. They have to organize the information in that database on certain principles Sachs gives them, and they have to ensure that the details do, in fact, support their argument.

Drawing from the work of various researchers who study the effects of teaching thinking skills explicity, I believe teachers systematically should ask middle school students to practice specific thinking skills. Students need to be able to define and clarify problems; the way in which a problem is articulated affects the choices of strategies used to solve it. In order to be able to state a problem appropriately, students

**Figure 5–2**
Focus Paper Overview

---

FOCUS PAPER: DO I DARE DISTURB THE UNIVERSE?
PROTAGONIST CHARACTER DEVELOPMENTS CHART

DIRECTIONS: Select one major quality (characteristic) of the protagonist. Cite events of statements from the story that provide evidence
that the protagonist has this quality. Be sure to find examples reflective
of the four methods an author can use to develop his/her characters.
In the boxes below, write the page numbers on which you found
examples.

| Directly stated by author | Actions of character | What character says | What others say about protagonist |
|---|---|---|---|
| Page # Examples | Page # Examples | Page # Examples | Page # Examples |

need to be able to identify central issues involved in the problematic
situation. Additionally, they need to be able to define their terms, and
to identify assumptions, biases, stereotypes, and underlying ideologies.
They need to be able to collect data, determine whether or not it is
related to and adequate for helping to find solutions, brainstorm possible interpretations and solutions, and select the best possible one to fit
the scenario.

Underlying these skills are other, more discrete skills, such as listing, attending to detail, observing, classifying, and summarizing. For
example, to organize data, students may have to create and interpret

charts and graphs, order or sequence data, and use numbers as well as words to capture their observations.

Furthermore, there are affective skills required in the development of a particular response to a situation. For instance, they will have to tolerate ambiguity, live with incomplete closure, defer judgment, and appreciate the need for nonconformity and a diversity of perspectives. Perhaps most important, they will have to recognize that the solution to one problem frequently gives rise to another; evaluation of the process and product are cyclical and crucial elements of both creative and critical thinking.

Many states are moving away from the use of tests that assess student knowledge and skill in discrete chunks or that assess generalized cognitive ability. California assesses critical thinking, examining students' abilities to define and clarify a problem, judge information related to the problem, and solve it (Kneedler 1985). During the Maryland State Performance Assessment Program, Maryland students have to participate in both individual and cooperative tasks designed to assess their abilities:

to write in a variety of genres for a variety of purposes about topics that cross content-area boundaries;

to make inferences;

to justify responses;

to use prior knowledge and personal experience in comparison with ideas expressed in texts;

to revisit texts of various kinds for various purposes;

to relate subject matter from one content area to others.

They also are asked to describe *how* they think through problems; metacognitive skill is increasingly required of these students.

When implementing transdisciplinary units based on young adult texts, it is almost impossible to avoid engaging students in the kind of complex thinking demanded by new assessment procedures—and by our increasingly complex world. Just consider how many skills adults need in order to reach their place of employment each day. Driving from home to work requires reading and cooperating skills—predicting what other motorists will do, responding to traffic situations accordingly, following the rules of the road, engaging in the give and take of rush hour driving—time estimation skills, observation skills, and motor skills (eye/hand/foot coordination), none of which is practiced during schooling in one specific content area.

How, in general, do we learn the skills necessary for survival in everyday life? What different skills are required for survival in situations out of the realm of ordinary experience—from traveling in a foreign country to being lost in the wilderness? What different skills for survival will be required by the generations to come? A fairly routine activity such as driving to work demonstrates the transdisciplinary nature of the thinking skills required for surviving long enough to move from home to work in the morning. Good readers naturally have to engage in these same kinds of tasks—organizing time, predicting, reacting to others' actions/responses, observing, comparing/contrasting, evaluating, etc.—it makes sense, then, to require engagement with texts as the heart of transdisciplinary teaching.

Consider Maxwell from *Freak the Mighty* (Roderick 1993). Max, who has always been in LD classes and who has never been successful as a reader, finally learns to make sense out of print when his friend Kevin tells him, "words are just voices on papers. . . . reading is just another way of listening, and I could always listen" (82). Good readers have to use their prior knowledge and prior experiences—as Kevin tells Maxwell—to make sense of words and contexts with which they are unfamiliar. They have to observe and keep track of plot and character details in order to maintain a sense of continuity; they often make predictions about what will happen based on those observations; and they compare themselves and their experiences to the lives of the characters or to the worlds described in nonfiction texts. If the author is slow to hook the reader into the plot, or if the characters initially seem uninteresting or the material at first does not seem relevant to the task at hand, the reader has to suspend judgment, skimming until enough data is in hand to justify either continuing to read or putting the book aside. If the author is slowly building an argument, step-by-step, the reader will have to tolerate the process and trust the writer's ability to deliver what he or she has promised. Readers ultimately evaluate whether the text was worth the time they spent reading it given their purpose for doing so.

For example, in the unit "There's No Place Like Home" (Chapter 2), students begin their study of home by examining their intuitive definition of the concept. Gradually, they add data to their knowledge base through their experiences with many different literary works about characters whose life experiences may be quite foreign to their own and may be shaped by very different cultural contexts. They elaborate on this concept by using the term "home" as do experts in various fields: the computer programmer, the social worker, the historian or archaeologist, the scientist. As they acquire more knowledge, they have to compare and contrast these perspectives through analyzing the various specific instances of the use of the concept—

especially as it differs in fictional and nonfictional contexts—in order, eventually, to create a generalized definition of home that applies across the board.

While students in the "Home" unit are engaged in collecting data, they have to tolerate points of view that differ from their own, and they have to think creatively about how best to express their developing understanding of home to their peers. Ultimately, these students should have a better sense of how they are connected to all humanity, as home is a concept that transcends cultural boundaries, and they should have a better understanding of what kind of ideal home they want and can realistically work to achieve.

## Inquiry, Multiple Texts, and a Reader Response Approach to Literature

### *Inquiry*

What does "inquiry" mean when used to describe a systematic curricular structure? Teachers frequently confuse the terms *discovery learning* and *inquiry*. While they share some elements—including the basic premise that students learn more and are more motivated to do so when they are active participants in the learning process—discovery learning typically involves more teacher direction of that process. Generally, teachers using the discovery method identify a problem for students to investigate, provide the necessary resources for conducting the investigation, and help students arrive at conclusions that teachers usually have already identified.

In a true inquiry-based classroom, the students help articulate the problem to be investigated and help to generate the methods of investigation. For example, in *The Fire Bug Connection* (George 1993), Maggie receives a collection of exotic and beautiful fire bugs as a birthday present. They are supposed to change from adolescents to adults through a dramatic molting process. But some of Maggie's bugs shed their fifth coats without developing wings; they become grossly large and then die. Maggie decides to find out what is going on. With the help of a computer whiz, Mitch, she generates numerous hypotheses—from holes in the ozone layer to contaminated food supplies—that she tests out by gathering information from networked databases, interviewing workers at the local paper plant, and conducting experiments.

Eventually, Maggie figures out that there is a juvenile hormone in the balsam fir tree that kills the bugs; the paper lining of their container was made from the fir. Maggie and Mitch identify the problem, identify ways to solve it, and identify a solution without help from a teacher in any formal sense. Their parents, all scientists, give them some tips and encourage their thinking, but never appropriate the investigation, although they do ask questions, such as "Have you thought about . . . ?" The teacher is a *partner* in the inquiry process, which leads all of the participants to the discovery of conclusions not necessarily anticipated or known by the teacher. Even Maggie's and Mitch's parents are as surprised and awed by the results as the children are.

The basic elements of inquiry as demonstrated by Maggie and Mitch, which are the basis for teaching and learning, include doubting, clarifying, hypothesizing, reasoning, testing, and concluding. Traugh (1974) poses a series of questions to ask in order to ensure that programs and materials are faithful to these elements of inquiry, which I find to be a useful starting point for planning:

1. Are there questions, visual aids, and other devices that will lead to problem posing?

2. Are there means provided which allow for student exploration of the problem?

3. Are students called upon to analyze their explanations and hypotheses?

4. Are there means by which students can test and reformulate their hypotheses?

5. Are there materials available that help students move toward synthesis of the situation?

6. Are the processes and terms defined, and are definitions used consistently throughout the inquiry? (202)

In general, participation in inquiry is an effective means of developing students' abilities as systematic, symbolic thinkers. Andrews (1989), analyzing the value of inquiry for preservice teachers in a language arts methods class, notes the cyclical nature of inquiry; data collection and the development of the next phase of the curriculum are both significant junctures at which new inquiry may arise.

Planning for transdisciplinary, inquiry-based classrooms is problematic, and even scary for some teachers because it is difficult to predict how a year of study, or even one unit, might unfold. Chapters 2, 3, and 4 illustrate this difficulty. I can provide sample questions and tasks, and I can annotate sample text sets, but I cannot propose answers for the various questions suggested in these chapters; students in different classrooms working at different points in time out of different social contexts will arrive at different answers. And the assumption underlying the description of the text sets is that teachers and students together will determine which ones seem most likely to promote reflection. Teachers totally committed to participating in inquiry with their students will allow a great deal of the decision making—even about the questions to be explored and the texts to be read—to rest in students' hands.

## Multiple Texts

True inquiry begins with disequilibrium, with a discrepant event that creates surprise and curiosity. The use of multiple texts, which can provide students with discrepancies, and the belief that reader response theory allows for significant engagement with those texts by readers seeking to deal with those discrepancies, are, therefore, key ingredients of a transdisciplinary curriculum designed to promote true inquiry. Additionally, using multiple texts and inviting reader response to them helps teachers avoid some of the pitfalls of inquiry as outlined by Cornbleth (1978). Analyzing problems that arise in the implementation of an inquiry-based curriculum, she notes failure to build upon *student*-generated questions, to individualize, and to teach students how to transfer inquiry practice into use in the world outside the classroom as the three major difficulties in programs and materials she studied, including the Harvard Social Studies Project/Public Issues Series and the Taba Program in Social Science.

Use of the single-text approach assumes that students will be equally able readers, will respond equally well to a given text, and will read at the same pace. But teachers face increasingly large classes filled with students of diverse abilities and interests; thus, motivation, skill, and interest level in any one text are likely to vary widely. Using multiple texts helps overcome these differences.

Imdieke (1992) describes in detail how she uses characters from a piece of time-travel fiction as "historical guides." By interacting with these characters who have traveled in other times, students are led to inquire about the nature of time-travel literature, to investigate other examples of that genre, to research historical texts reflective of various time periods, and to discover related math, science, art, and music skills through diverse media. The Root Cellar (1983) by Janet Lunn is the springboard from which Imdieke's students plunge into a rich, transdisciplinary exploration of multiple concepts. In the novel, twelve-year-old orphan Rose is sent to live with her unknown relatives in Canada. When she ventures into her aunt's root cellar, she meets the people who lived on the farm more than a century earlier. Imdieke uses Lunn's novel to provoke discussion, question asking, and problem posing. As students compare and contrast the novel with nonfiction works and with visual media presentations about the time period of *The Root Cellar*, discrepancies, doubt about authenticity, and questions about historical fiction and how to read it arise, leading students into true inquiry.

In my Young Adult Literature course (designed for preservice English teachers and library-media specialists), I often set texts against each other to promote reflection both on what they have to say and on how they work that does not seem to arise when we talk about one book in isolation. In the local school districts surrounding the university, several books by Katherine Paterson are "taught"; that is, groups of students all read the same title at the same time, answering questions, role playing scenes, writing journal entries and papers, and making presentations on it as the "unit" progresses. *The Great Gilly Hopkins* (1978), *Bridge to Terabithia* (1977), *Jacob Have I Loved* (1980), *Park's Quest* (1988), and *Sign of the Chrysanthemum* (1973) are used in various locales nearby. To help my students develop some knowledge of the material with which they may be expected to work when they leave the campus and enter public school classrooms, I ask them to choose one of these titles to read during the course of the semester.

During the class session devoted to Paterson, students engage in a jigsaw strategy. First, all the readers of the same text meet together to refresh their memories about character names, ages, and relationships; plot events; settings; and themes. This step in the lesson is crucial because they are reading many books simultaneously for other courses, and they read over twenty young adult titles for this class, so their Paterson text may not be fresh in their minds. They have an opportunity to discuss how they felt about the text; I might ask them to share with the group how they resemble or differ from the main character, or to identify the one passage in the book that "stuck" in their minds or hearts.

Next, I regroup them so that each new group contains readers of at least four different Paterson titles. Initially, group members tell one another about their chosen titles, using their prior discussions with other readers of the same text as a guide. Then, they begin to engage in inquiry. I provide a catalyst for their discussion. Sometimes I ask them to name a unit and provide goals for it that would encompass all the titles—and the unit cannot be called "Katherine Paterson." Other times I read them a section from one of her essays in *Gates of Excellence* (1981), in which she articulates a theme that permeates her work. Once I pointed out that Cormier's Jerry Renault spends all of *The Chocolate War* (1974) trying to decide, "Do I dare disturb the universe?" and that Paterson has titled one of her speeches with that same phrase. Upon occasion, I have asked them to become a main character from the work they read and then to talk, as that character, about a topic such as honor or love or what it means to be an outsider.

During the fall semester of the 1994–1995 academic year, I wandered from group to group writing down the questions that emerged as the group members shared their texts and tried to synthesize their individual knowledge of Paterson with their increasing understanding of her work as a whole developed through the group process. Following are some of the more provocative questions that emerged and maintained students' interest and participation as they struggled to determine answers:

1. How has Paterson's personal history affected what she writes about, where she sets her books, and how she crafts her novels?

2. Does Paterson hold conventional Christian beliefs and, if so, does she intend to help her readers explore concepts such as grace and mercy?

3. Would it be possible to capture the multiple layers of meaning of Paterson's texts on video or using other nonprint media?

4. Do Paterson's other books support the hypothesis that "the outsider" is a key motif in her work?

5. Why did the male members of the group have more trouble relating to the texts and express more criticism of Paterson's writing than the female members of the group?

6. How do younger readers respond to Paterson's works, since they seem to have complex characters and difficult themes, and especially since they often end on what could be perceived as an unhappy note?

Consideration of the *collection* of titles represented in each group moved the students into the kind of synthesis and evaluation reflected in these questions in a way that did not happen when they considered the works in isolation. The expert group that read *Bridge to Terabithia*, for instance, did discuss the possible symbolism of the bridge and of Jesse's decision, after Leslie's death, to invite May Belle into the kingdom he and Leslie had created. But it was considering this title against the backdrop of the others that prompted students to ask questions about Paterson's religious beliefs.

As students pondered their questions, they began to discuss ways to gather relevant information. One group decided that each member would search out and watch at least one movie version of Paterson's novels. When they returned the next week, they shared their observations, and then got into a discussion about how authors of books for young adults and directors of movies for that age group seem to have differing perceptions of what adolescents can handle. Two students then determined to do a final project for the course that involved comparing movie and book versions of young adult titles, learning about visual literacy, and attempting to make their own video based on the first chapter of *Jacob Have I Loved*. Two women in the group that raised the issue of adolescent response to Paterson's titles decided to scrap their initial ideas for a final project and to work together to devise a survey for middle school students about their reading habits and interests.

The point is that reading texts in juxtaposition to one another provides a shifting frame of reference against which students can respond to any one text. As the pool of available information widens and leads to an increased ability to hypothesize, students are ever more likely to experience the sense of surprise or disequilibrium that guides them into further inquiry.

### Reader Response

Similarly, discussing responses to a text with readers of the same text, or other texts dealing with the same theme or concept, also provides opportunities for the doubt and questioning necessary for inquiry. Ivy and Rodney from Okimoto's *Talent Night* (1995) are told by their English teacher to discuss their reactions to two stories: "I Sing the Body Electric" by Ray Bradbury and "The Very Old Man with Enormous Wings" by Gabriel Garcia Marquez. At first, Ivy says she liked the Bradbury title, but "it sure seems different than the other one ["The Very Old Man with Enormous Wings"], though" (31). So they decide to list the differences in the stories. As they talk, their ideas about the two stories become clearer—and they learn about each other, as well. After Rodney notes that the author of the "weird angel" story wrote it in Spanish, Ivy reveals that, because her last name is Ramos, people assume she speaks Spanish. This leads the two teenagers into a personal discussion about their shared experiences of the difficulties of being *hapa*—of mixed heritage.

The next time they meet to discuss the stories, they start by continuing that personal discussion. Ivy describes how, as one of six children, she frequently feels "lost" in her family, as if nobody has time for her. Thus she has responded to the Bradbury piece because she can appreciate the benefits an "electric grandmother" would have. Rodney, to this point, has not really made sense of the story or connected with it. Ivy then asks Rodney to read certain passages aloud because "I like to hear the words. I can think better that way" (40). Rodney tells us, "It seemed a little strange that she wanted me to read it out loud, but if she thought it was the best way for us to do the project, who was I to object?" (40). And so he reads—all the while watching Ivy's reaction to the text, which describes how each person in the family will be able to receive the electric grandmother's undivided attention. When he is done, Ivy says, "Isn't that wonderful? Don't you wish there was such a thing as an electric grandmother?" (42). And Rodney replies, understanding both Bradbury's concept and Ivy's reaction, "It'd be awesome" (42).

It is not until Rodney hears Ivy's interpretation of the story that he finds a way to connect to it; eventually, as a result of their discussions, the concept of "the electric grandmother" becomes a metaphor in their conversations about their own families and about life in general.

Reader response theory assumes that inquiry will occur when a reader interacts with a text. As Probst puts it in *Response and Analysis* (1988),

> When literature is *read* rather than worked upon, it draws us into events and invites us to reflect upon our perceptions of them. It is not at that point a subject to be studied as an artifact illustrating an age or a product representing an artist; it is rather an experience to be entered into. "Entering into" literature, however, may be different from most of our other experiences. The literary work invites us in not only as participants, but also as spectators, giving us the opportunity to watch ourselves. It freezes events and holds them still for thought; events move too quickly and we are too deeply and thoroughly involved. Literature, however, allows us both to experience and reflect upon experience, and thus invites the self-indulgence of those who seek to understand themselves and the world. (4)

It might be possible for a teacher or team of teachers to devise a unit with a young adult novel at its core that included content from disciplines other than English and did not allow for reader response to the text. For example, Chapter 3 describes the ways in which *Gulf* by Westall includes content references from multiple disciplines. The *teacher* could decide that students should, in fact, learn about those topics. The teacher could devise segments of instruction about language and how British and American "English" differ, the history of architecture, or the cultural and physical geography of Iraq, all while moving through the book, chapter by chapter, using study guides to check students' understanding of the basic elements of the story. However, a unit so planned would *not* truly be transdisciplinary in nature; students would *not* be enhancing their concept of "conflict" by exploring it from multiple perspectives, and they certainly would *not* be practicing inquiry skills.

Literature, when reader response is allowed and encouraged, helps us not only to expand our view of the world, but to rethink our own place in it and our relationship to it and to others as well. Thus,

Rosenblatt argues that discussion of a text has to begin as the reader articulates his or her response to the text. This response is not necessarily "right," but it has to be the starting point for dealing with the text because the reader's response is reflective of the past history of the reader as well as of the intersection of the text with that history. As a group of readers shares responses, the individual group members begin to question why the text has affected them differently from others in the group. They can uncover their personal biases and value structures and they can pull their knowledge of the writer's craft to create a deeper collective appreciation of how the text "works" to cause various responses to it. They can begin to compare themselves to the kind of reader for whom the author had hoped, and they can move into consideration of how the circumstances in which an author wrote affected the various choices he or she made while writing.

From a reader response-based perspective, a text is never "static." An author may have carefully chosen language and details for very specific reasons understandable to his or her contemporaries. However, readers interacting with that text in another place and time will bring a different lens to bear on it, opening it up to different interpretations and meanings—and hence allowing for the possibility of transdisciplinary inquiry in ways that other approaches to text do not.

## Assessment and Transdisciplinary Curricular Planning

If students help to organize their own learning, if language processing and thinking skills are emphasized as well as content, if students read multiple texts to which they respond in differing ways, if concepts are explored through a variety of perspectives that synthesize the traditional disciplines into a larger whole, then it will be difficult not only to construct but to justify the standard "unit test" as the primary assessment tool. The professional literature is filled with calls for more "authentic" assessment than that which students have traditionally experienced, and even the Educational Testing Service, that bastion of quantitative psychometricians, has begun to reflect on the limitations of standard, and standardized, assessment tools.

What is "authentic assessment"? In general, the term implies that assessment and learning are intertwined. Sometimes referred to as aligned, accurate, or alternative assessment, authentic assessment involves a commitment to use a variety of strategies to determine whether students are meeting instructional objectives (Meyer 1992). Regular classroom instruction and the tasks related to it are viewed as assessment tools. Every activity related to the curricular goals in which students engage, either inside or outside the classroom, provides, from the "authentic assessment" perspective, an opportunity for both teacher and students to reflect on growth, to evaluate what has been learned and mastered and what still is left to accomplish.

Because "authentic assessment" implies a cyclical view of evaluation in that students constantly self-assess and then set new goals, it is clearly related to the inquiry cycle in which learning constantly leads to questioning, which leads to more learning, and so on. Even the process of setting standards by which to assess progress becomes an opportunity for collaboration, compromise, reflection, and inquiry. As Kritt (1993) notes, developing consensus about performance standards is a truly challenging task that demands higher-level thinking on the part of students. He also argues that reflective self-evaluation should be an integral part of every classroom assignment and lesson, not an obligatory afterthought.

The April 1995 issue of *Voices in the Middle* contains a collection of articles on the reading process which provide models of how to incorporate self-evaluation into a text-based classroom. Crowley (1995) describes the value for Gregg, a middle school student who perceived himself as a failed reader, of learning to self-assess his own miscues. Eventually, Gregg began to realize that "*he* is responsible for getting his reading to make sense and, if it doesn't sound like language, it can't make sense" (7). Crowley also describes the importance of modeling reading self-evaluation for his students and sharing with them strategies they can use to overcome problems with texts. Wright (1995) also shows how her students grow as readers when, as part of the normal classroom routine, they have to "gain an accurate perspective on the reading process and on themselves as readers" (22) through explicit discussion of their reading strategies and self-evaluation, with the teacher's assistance, of their strengths as readers.

Treu (1995) details her use of double-entry journals as both a part of the normal set of expectations she has of her middle school English students as they read young adult novels, and a window through which she can assess their interaction with texts. She has found, as a result, that her students, whose oral language and home experience is much different from the language of books, frequently say, "I don't know!" when asked what they think about a text because they truly *don't* know what to make of it. On the other hand, the double-entry journals, in which students copy passages that "stick" with them, have shown her that "eighth graders are naturally attracted to beautiful language. . . . Clearly, I had underestimated my students' capacity to respond deeply to their reading" (33). She found that students often copied the poetic passages from Sebestyen's *Words by Heart* (1968), even when unsure of their meaning. At other times, students' comments about the passages reflect that they are reading word-for-word and not finding meaning in the context—thus allowing Treu to review what constitutes good reading and to remind them of the strategies for meaning making they already know.

These teachers recognize the difference between measurement, the collecting of quantifiable data about students' behaviors, skills, and knowledge, and assessment, the collecting of multiple forms of data that allows the collector to arrive at a well-rounded value judgment about the student's performance relative to the learning objectives. In general, teachers can examine and reflect on what students say, what they write, what they produce using other media, and what they do in various contexts and situations. Transdisciplinary classrooms consistently provide opportunities for students to use the tools of multiple disciplines and to participate in diverse activities reflecting multiple ways to explore a problem or issue. Therefore, teachers in such classrooms are uniquely poised to engage in authentic assessment. And, when creating an inquiry environment in which to help students set the agenda for their learning and establish criteria for assessing it, transdisciplinary text-based teachers can help their *students* become practiced at authentic assessment.

Here is a list "from A to Z" of possible projects, products, and more standard tools of evaluation that can be used together to provide a basis for authentic assessment. Individual teachers can imagine how best to use these options. For example, a teacher might ask students to generate a list of bumper stickers they have seen that character *x* might have on his car, or she might ask students to create a bumper sticker slogan to summarize some concept they have studied. As a way of self evaluating, students might create resumes; or they could create a resume for a character whom they have studied.

A.  Anagrams, autobiographies (real and fictional), advertisements (using various media), analyses, arguments (verbal and written), agendas

B.  Bumper stickers, billboards, battle cries, biographies, "best of" lists, Bingo variations, ballads, book talks

C.  Children's stories, cartoons, captions, comic strips, collections, collages, choral readings, crossword puzzles, charts, cross-section illustrations, classified ads, charades, conferences, checklists, creative dramatics

D.  Demonstrations, dioramas, dramatic monologues, diaries, dictation, dialogue journals, dialogues, detail charts, directions, decision-making charts, descriptions, debates, discussion, dances

E.  Experiments, editorials, essays, epitaphs, epigrams, eulogies, encyclopedia entries, "essentials" lists

F.  Filmstrips, "found" poetry, fairy tales, fact files, fill-in-the-blank items, family trees, flip books, fiction

G.  Glossary, games, graffiti, goals, greeting cards, grocery lists, graphs, guidelines, generalizations

H.  Haiku, humorous speeches/stories/poems, hidden pictures, "how-tos," homework

I.  Indexes, interviews, insults, interior monologues, illustrations, imitations (in writing, in performance), inquiry letters

J.  Jigsaw puzzles, jokes, journals, jump rope jingles, jazz accompaniments, "jelly-fish" graphic organizers, Jeopardy

K.  Kernel sentences, kites, kits, K/W/L lists

L.  Labels, limericks, let's pretend . . . , letters, large-scale diagrams, lists of various sorts, lab reports, laws, labs

M.  Maps, metaphors, museum exhibits, models, monographs, murals, memos, menus, mobiles, "matching" and "multiple choice" items, musical accompaniments, mock trials

N.  Newspapers, notebooks, news stories

O.  Operas/operettas, observation logs, one-act plays, onomatopoeia, outlines, oral reports, "Odyssey of the Mind"

P.  Plays, patterns, pamphlets, poems, picture dictionaries, pictures, posters, puppets/puppet shows, protest songs, petitions, paragraph frames, persuasive speeches, prayers, "personals," principles, peer evaluations

Q.  Questions, queries, quintessential sayings, quotes, quizzes

R.  Rebus stories, rhymed verse, research, recordings, riddles, raps, races, resumes, rules, role plays

S.  Scavenger hunts, sketches, slide-tape shows, stream of consciousness, satire, songs, stencils, stories, surveys, street maps, sentence starters, sculptures, science fiction, speeches, skits, story chains, survival manuals, self-assessment survey, simulations

T.  Tests, tapes, telegrams, TV scripts, terrariums, textbooks, transparencies, travelogues, Trivial Pursuit,® tall tales

U.  Unrhymed verse, underground newspaper

V.  Verse, videos, vocabulary lists, vitae, Venn diagrams, visual displays

W.  Worksheets, westerns, word pictures, word problems, want ads, written reports

X. "Xeroxing" (imitations of others' work), X-rays (identifying the supporting structure underneath a text, play, or other product)

Y. Young adult fiction, yes/no questions (for "Twenty Questions")

Z. Zeugmas, zany anecdotes, zippy comebacks, zoo exhibits.

(synthesized from Stover, Neubert, and Lawlor 1993, 96–97; vanAllen 1994)

Any individual writing assignment, product, or performance can become part of a larger authentic assessment tool—the student portfolio. Portfolios are collections of both artifacts and written reflections chosen by the student as reflective of personal growth and progress, or of "best effort," at a certain point in time. The student is responsible for organizing the items in the portfolio; more sophisticated students can determine their own organizing principles while students less practiced in the art of portfolio making will require some guidance. In general, artifacts, classwork, homework, projects, writing samples, self-evaluation forms, and peer evaluations (such as those peers might complete on a writing assignment, or those group members complete after working together in a group) might be found in a portfolio.

Additionally, teachers should guide students through the writing of an introductory statement, describing what is included and why it was chosen for inclusion, and a reflective piece at the conclusion, detailing what the student has learned from engaging in the portfolio process. It is useful, at least initially, to guide students in the writing of this reflective piece by asking them to answer specific questions, such as

1. How are you doing overall compared to the last time you did a self-evaluation?

2. How successful are you in terms of taking responsibility for completing assignments on time? (Consider homework, classwork, projects, writing assignments, reading assignments.)

3. How would you evaluate, on a scale of one to ten, how much you are learning in this class? (A useful variation on this item is to ask students to complete, five different times, a sentence such as "I used to think (or believe, know, feel) _____ about _____ , but now I think (or believe, know, feel) _____ because _____ ." They can use different verbs for different sentences or at different points in the sentence.)

4. What could you do to improve your performance? What could the teacher do?

5. What objectives for the class do you think you've successfully met? What do you still need to accomplish?

6. Describe at least one situation outside of this classroom when you've used something you've learned in it.

7. What do you like best about your portfolio?

8. How well do you think you are getting along with your peers?

9. What thinking skills have you practiced most since your last self-evaluation?

10. What goals do you have for the next X days/weeks/units, etc.

As the teacher prepares to confer with the student about the portfolio, he or she might complete the following sentences:

a. I think you show strengths in _____ because _____ .
b. I think you could work on _____ because _____ .
c. My favorite part of your portfolio was _____ because _____ .
d. You show growth in _____ because _____ .
e. Other comments:

Ideally, middle school teachers will take a lesson from their students and will develop the habit of reflecting on their practice both individually and as members of transdisciplinary teams. Christenson, in Christenson and Carroll (1995), provides a model for this kind of reflective practice when she writes,

> As students learned to evaluate their progress, I was encouraged to evaluate my own. I sat down with the class during self-reflection sessions and thought about my own growth. I recognized that I had accomplished some of my goals, but not others. I was reading different types of literature and using other authors as resources to help me with my own writing. I was doing more personal reading and writing . . .
>
> Setting and accomplishing goals not only helped me learn how to be a better reader and writer, but it also gave me more confidence. That confidence helped my teaching. I felt I now understood and could teach students about different writing styles and techniques. In addition, I could talk with conviction about personal growth as reader and writer. (49)

## Conclusion

Fictional teachers like Ms. Finney and Alice's brother Lester and real teachers such as Karr, Sachs, Imdieke, and Christenson share many of the characteristics I hope to see develop in the preservice teachers with whom I work. They understand motivation theory, use bridges, integrate all the language-processing skills, attend to the development of thinking skills, use multiple texts, promote inquiry and reflection, recognize the value of young adult literature as a basis for planning and wisdom of reader response theory, and employ authentic assessment practices. In general, they would all be comfortable calling themselves "whole language" teachers. The principles of the whole language movement undergird this entire text, and it is the philosophical starting point for my argument that young adult literature should be at the heart of trandisciplinary middle school curricula.

Kenneth Goodman (1986) defines whole language by saying,

> Whole language is an attempt to get back to basics in the real sense of that word—to set aside basals, workbooks, and texts, and to return to inviting kids to learn to read and write by reading and writing real stuff. (38)

Hal Foster (1994) states,

> To some extent, whole language both competes with and complements the traditional triad. Whole language is the gathering in of all the personal-growth theories from the fields of writing, reading, literacy theory, educational psychology, even anthropology and semiotics. Whole language doesn't condemn the teaching of Western civilization, but the emphasis is different. Whole language emphasizes the importance of considering the student and his/her needs. Whole language considers the process of education, as well as the products. (10)

Frank Smith (1992) summarizes what these authors are saying when he states that the teacher who believes in whole language has a different way of thinking about teaching than the teacher who does not. Because the whole language teacher defines teaching differently, when a visitor enters the classroom of a teacher who has embraced the whole language philosophy, he or she is likely to see some of the activities listed below taking place, all of which embody what these authors say about that belief structure:

- students talking together in small groups or with partners, using spoken language to wrestle with an issue or answer a question;
- teacher and students engaging in "uninterrupted, sustained silent reading" of books freely chosen;
- students acting out stories they have read or using creative dramatics as a way to go public with their own writing;

- students writing based on their own need to put words on paper or computer screen as a way to make their thoughts and emotions visible, as a means of self-expression, and as a way of enhancing their learning processes—writing journals, writing notes to each other, writing a class newspaper, writing a script for the film they plan to videotape, writing response papers, writing questions they want others to answer, writing to friends around the world using e-mail/internet connections as they conduct primary-source research, writing a collaborative poem about the chapter they have just discussed from the book they all read;

- students making decisions about how class time will be spent;

- students deciding how they will show that they have grown as readers, writers, speakers, and listeners.

In general, in whole language classrooms, teachers create an environment in which both spoken and written language is used in ways meaningful to the students. Students and their needs and interests are at the heart of a whole language classroom, which is a place where they use language to make order out of chaos, to clarify what they already know, and to construct new meaning.

At the elementary level, teachers who have read Smith and Goodman do whatever they can to provide students with "wholes." They offer students whole texts read in one sitting and swallowed in one piece—opportunities to create whole texts themselves rather than fill in the blanks of someone else's text, and opportunities to engage in whole conversations with each other and with people outside the classroom rather than provide one-word factual responses to questions posed by the teacher.

Similarly, the whole language teacher at the middle school level will allow students to read whole novels, plays, and stories rather than always chopping up a lengthy text into chunks processed with "study questions." And he or she will allow students opportunities to debate their responses to those texts orally and in writing rather than demanding they complete exercises in a grammar book. Also, the whole language teacher understands the underlying nature of the work of social philosophers such as Paulo Freire. Working in third-world countries with illiterate adults, Freire documented the ways in which access to reading and writing affected their political and moral understanding of the world. In books such as *The Pedagogy of the Oppressed* (1970) and *The Politics of Education* (1985), Freire describes how the ability to use language empowers the language user, acting as a force for the user to be liberated from the limitations of externally imposed exploitation and internally imposed fears and misunderstandings.

Other sociologists of curriculum (Apple 1979; Giroux 1983), argue that no curriculum is neutral. All curricula reflect the particular view of society held by the writers. As Auerbach and Burgess (1987) write,

> This "hidden curriculum" generates social meanings, restraints, and cultural values that shape students' roles outside the classroom. The choices that educators make reflect their views of the learning process, the social context for learning, and the students' place in society. These choices have a very real impact on students: Giroux (1983) argues that the failure to examine assumptions about how particular materials mediate meanings between students, teachers, and society very often leaves little room for students to generate their own meanings and develop critical thinking. (150–151)

As scary as it seems, whole language teachers understand that their beliefs about teaching and learning may bring them into conflict with the traditional structures of public education in America. Their principles are grounded in a realization that education is about politics. As Freire writes,

> This is a great discovery, education is politics! When a teacher discovers that he or she is a politician, too, the teacher has to ask, What kind of politics am I doing in the classroom? That is, in favor of whom am I being a teacher? The teacher works in favor of something and against something. Because of that, he or she will have another great question, How to be consistent in my teaching practice with my political choice? I cannot proclaim my liberating dream and in the next day be authoritarian in my relationship with the students. (Shor 1987, preface)

Whole language teachers in the middle school who begin to plan transdisciplinary units based on young adult texts will recognize the implications of recent research about the nature of language development, and about reading and writing instruction, as well as about the hidden messages embedded in decisions about curriculum and instruction.

I want my own daughter to have teachers who will recognize and build on students' natural curiosity, and who will realize that helping students work together on real tasks, for real purposes (as defined, at least in part, by the students) will promote their growth as readers, writers, speakers, listeners, and thinkers. When I walk into the classrooms of my student teachers, I hope they will be "text rich" and thus likely to promote growth in literacy and the development of a reading habit, and I want to be able to tell that my student teachers see themselves as facilitators for students' efforts to make meaning rather than as disseminators of information and drillers of skills. The chart in Figure

5–3 illustrates in part the difference between the whole language teacher and the "less-whole-language-oriented" teacher. I want to see such practices in place.

I am not opposed to direct, teacher-led instruction. My daughter's reading skill improved after she was taught about the "magic *e*" on the end of a word that usually indicates the preceding vowel has a long sound. Systematic, direct instruction with manipulatives was responsible for her ability to understand and perform multiplication and division this past year, just as it was helpful during drama camp when the directors taught the campers concepts such as "stage left" and effective make-up. But it is the practice of such skills, as Amanda reads a script and rehearses her lines, that has led her to see the value of what she has learned through more traditional instructional means.

The early years of adolescence are not easy for anyone involved, not for students nor for their teachers nor for their parents. Students in grades five to eight are "in the middle," as Atwell terms them, in so many ways. Torn between being children and being adults, placed between elementary and high school, they need to feel secure in their classrooms so that they can get ready for the world of possibilities ahead of them as they reflect on the past and experience the tumultuous present. Transdisciplinary planning centered on young adult literature provides the kind of grounding middle school students deserve. A young adult text, accessible in its reflection of the emotional realities of middle grade students, provides something solid and tangible onto which to hold, from which to hypothesize and dream, on which to test out possible selves and through which to learn about others. I hope my daughter and her peers have teachers who value the power of literature and who believe in the possibilities of transdisciplinary connections and authentic assessment inherent in its use. I hope her teachers know the truth of what Probst writes at the very end of *Response and Analysis* (1988) when he says that the *reader* is

> at the center of the literary experience, thus redefining literature's place in the culture. It becomes once more again the possession of everyman, rather than of the scholarly elite, and it provides him with a touchstone by which to judge and revise his own conceptions of the world and his place in it. It merits a place at the center of the curriculum, as the most fundamental and significant of all the disciplines, for it is in the study of literature that we each build the conceptual world in which we live. (253)

My hope is that teachers of middle school students will, by engaging them in transdisciplinary inquiry grounded in young adult literature, help them begin to understand that education can and should be about exploring the complexity of relationships that make up our individual and collective lives.

**Figure 5–3**

Comparison of Whole Language to Other Practices

| In whole language classrooms the teacher: | In other classrooms, the teacher: |
|---|---|
| 1) allows students to write about topics meaningful to them on a personal basis, providing ideas and assistance in selecting and narrowing when appropriate; | 1) selects the topics for writing or only offers students limited choices; |
| 2) understands that not all writing needs to be evaluated by the teacher; | 2) evaluates for "correctness" most of the writing students do; |
| 3) understands that not all students write best when seated at their desks and provides alternatives; | 3) assumes that all students can and will write when seated at their desks and when given time in class to write; |
| 4) allows students to explore diverse genres and to find their own voice as writers; | 4) structures students into certain genres when they are writing — "Today, we'll be working on poems," "Today we're writing comparison/contrast essays." |
| 5) provides forums for students who wish to go public with their work; | 5) is the sole audience for students' work and grades student work at home based on established criteria; |
| 6) conferences about work with students, helping them set goals for themselves and helping them to monitor their own progress; | 6) chooses goals for students and assesses their progress toward these goals; |
| 7) recognizes that there is not one writing process, but many; | 7) teaches "the writing process" and assumes it will be comfortable for every student; |
| 8) fosters interdisciplinary connections and plans for instruction which fosters connections among all the language processing skills; | 8) teaches content and skills in isolation from the rest of the curriculum and from each other; |

| | |
|---|---|
| 9) uses collaborative and cooperative instructional strategies; | 9) uses, primarily, whole-class instructional strategies and much direct instruction; |
| 10) allows students to make choices about the books they read and emphasizes the reading of whole texts; | 10) makes decisions about which books all students will read, or offers limited choices; |
| 11) encourages students' response to texts, recognizing that the text comes alive in a different way for each individual reader; | 11) focuses on an accepted interpretation of a text or asks for close analysis without building such analysis on student response; |
| 12) allows students to use art, music, drama, and other active ways for showing what they have learned; | 12) fails to honor multiple modes of knowing; |
| 13) engages parents in the classroom in diverse ways to help foster students' language use; | 13) is fearful of too much parental involvement; |
| 14) uses young adult literature in diverse ways; | 14) relies on the established "cannon" as the basis for the literature program; |
| 15) uses many kinds of print and nonprint materials; | 15) emphasizes traditional print materials; |
| 16) uses varied assessment procedures, including portfolio systems and project-based assessment plans. | 16) relies heavily on paper and pencil testing procedures. |

## Resources on Authentic/Portfolio Assessment

Note: "Portfolios" is the theme of the October 1994 (71:6) issue of *Language Arts*.

Abruscato, J. 1993. "Early Results and Tentative Implications from the Vermont Portfolio Project." *Phi Delta Kappan* 74(6): 474–77. (There are several useful articles about assessment in this issue.)

Calfee, R. C., K. L. Dunlap, and A. Y. Wat. 1994. "Authentic Discussion of Text in Middle Grade Schooling: An Analytic-Narrative Approach." *Journal of Reading* 37: 546–56.

Fried, C. S. 1993. "Evaluation, Reflection, Revision: Using Literature Discussion Groups in Middle School." In *Cycles of Meaning*, edited by K. Pierce and C. Giles. Portsmouth, NH: Heineman.

Gilbert, Judith C. 1994. *Portfolio Resource Guide: Creating and Using Portfolios in the Classroom*. Ottawa, KS: The Writing Project. (P. O. Box 664, Ottawa, KS.)

Goldman, J. P. 1989. "Student Portfolios Already Proven in Some Schools." *School Administrator* 46(11): 11.

Hamm, M., and D. Adams. 1991. "Portfolio Assessment in Science." *The Science Teacher* 58(5): 18–21.

Jongsma, J. K. 1989. "Portfolio Assessment." *Reading Teacher* 43(3): 264–65.

Lamme, L. L., and C. Hysmith. 1991. "One School's Adventure into Portfolio Assessment." *Language Arts* 68(8): 629–40.

McRobbie, Joan. 1992. *Using Portfolios to Assess Student Performance*. ERIC Document ED351378. Knowledge Brief #9.

McVeigh-Schultz, J. 1995. "Poetry and Assessment." *Language Arts* 72(1): 39–41.

Scott, J. E. 1994. "Literature Circles in the Middle School Classroom: Overlapping Reading, Responding, and Responsibility." *Middle School Journal* 26(2): 37–41.

Wiggins, G. 1993. "Assessment: Authenticity, Context, and Validity." *Phi Delta Kappan* 75(3): 200–14.

Wolf, D. P. 1989. "Portfolio Assessment: Sampling Student Work." *Educational Leadership* 46(7): 35–39.

# Resources on Cooperative Learning—Research and Strategies

Johnson, D., and R. Johnson. 1985. "Motivational Processes in Cooperative, Competitive, and Individualistic Learning Situations." In *Research on Motivation in Education*, Vol. 12, edited by C. Ames and R. Ames. New York: Academic Press.

Johnson, D., R. Johnson, E. Holubec, and P. Ray. 1984. *Circle of Learning: Cooperation in the Classroom*. Alexandria, VA: Association for Supervision and Curriculum Development.

Lyman, Frank, and H. C. Foyle. 1990. *Cooperative Groups for Interactive Learning*. Washington, DC: National Educational Association.

Slavin, Robert. 1980. "Effects of Student Teams and Peer Tutoring on Academic Achievement and Time on Task." *Journal of Experimental Education* 48: 252–57.

———. 1983. *Cooperative Learning*. New York: Longman.

———. 1984. "Students Motivating Students to Excel: Cooperative Incentives, Cooperative Tasks, and Student Achievement." *Elementary School Journal* 85: 53–64.

————. 1990. "Achievement Effects of Ability Grouping in Secondary Schools: A Best-Evidence Synthesis." *Review of Educational Research* 60: 471–500.

Slavin, R. E., N. L. Karweil, and N. A. Madden. 1989. *Effective Programs for Students at Risk*. Boston: Allyn and Bacon.

Shepard, David L. 1972. *Comprehensive High School Reading Methods*. Columbus, OH: Merrill. (Deals with grouping students for cooperative work.)

## Resources on Developing Thinking Skills

Costa, A. L., ed. 1985. *Developing Minds: A Resource Book for Teaching Thinking*. Alexandria, VA: Association for Supervision and Curriculum Development.

Marzano, Robert. 1993. *Assessing Student Performance*. Alexandria, VA: Association for Supervision and Curriculum Development.

Perkins, D. N. 1987. "Thinking Frames: An Integrative Perspective on Teaching Cognitive Skills." In *Teaching Thinking Skills: Theory and Practice*, edited by J. B. Baron and R. J. Sternberg. New York: Freeman.

## Resources on Inquiry

Goodman, Jesse. 1986. "Teaching Preservice Teachers a Critical Approach to Curriculum Design: A Descriptive Account." *Curriculum Theory* 16(2): 179–220.

Kim, Eugene C., and Richard D. Kellough. 1995. *A Resource Guide for Secondary School Teaching: Planning for Competence*, 6th ed. Englewood Cliffs, NJ: Merrill.

Taba, Hilda. 1969. *Teaching Strategies and Cognitive Functioning in Elementary School Children*. ERIC Document ED025448.

Zevin, Jack. 1969. "Today's Education." *National Education Association Journal* May: 42–43.

## Resources on Middle School Organization, Administration, and Practice

Berry, J. E., and J. Valentine. 1993. "The Organizational Structure of Effective Middle Schools." In *Middle School Research: Selected Studies, 1974–1993*, edited by D. B. Strahan. Columbus, OH: National Middle School Association.

Doda, Nancy. 1992. "Teaming: Its Burdens and Its Blessings." In *Connecting the Curriculum Through Interdisciplinary Instruction*, edited by J. Lounsbury. Columbus, OH: National Middle School Association.

George, P. S., and L. L. Oldaker. 1985. *Evidence for the Middle School.* Columbus, OH: National Middle School Association.

Lake, Sara. 1989. *Exploratory and Elective Courses in the Middle Level School.* Practitioner's Monograph #8. ERIC Document ED316914.

Levine, R. F., and E. Eubanks. 1984. "Characteristics of Successful Inner-City Intermediate Schools." *Phi Delta Kappan* 65: 707–11.

Lipsitz, J. 1984. *Successful Schools for Young Adolescents.* New Brunswick, NJ: Transaction Books.

Schumacher, Donna. 1992. "A Multiple Case Study of Curriculum Integration by Selected Middle School Interdisciplinary Teams of Teachers." Paper presented at the Annual Conference of the American Educational Research Association, San Francisco, April 20–24. ERIC Document ED356518.

## Resources on Motivation Theory

DeCharms, R. 1983. "Intrinsic Motivation, Peer Tutoring, and Cooperative Learning: Practical Maxims." In *Teacher and Student Perceptions: Implications for Learning,* edited by J. Levine and M. Wang. Hillsdale, NJ: Erlbaum.

Graham, S. 1991. "A Review of Attribution Theory in Achievement Contexts." *Educational Psychology Review* 3: 5–39.

Maslow, A. H. 1970. *Motivation and Personality.* 2d ed. New York: Harper and Row.

Paulman, R. G., and K. J. Kennelly. 1984. "Test Anxiety and Ineffective Test Taking: Different Names, Same Construct?" *Journal of Educational Psychology* 76: 279–88.

Purkey, W. W. 1978. *Inviting School Success.* Belmont, CA: Wadsworth.

Rotter, J. 1954. *Social Learning and Clinical Psychology.* Englewood Cliffs, NJ: Prentice Hall.

Tobias, Sigmund. 1985. "Text Anxiety: Interference, Defective Skills, and Cognitive Capacity." *Educational Psychologist* 20: 135–42.

Weiner, B. 1990. "History of Motivation Research in Education." *Journal of Educational Psychology* 82: 616–22.

## Resources on Reader Response Theory

Karolides, N. J. 1992. "The Transactional Theory of Literature." In *Reader Response in the Classroom: Evoking and Interpreting Meaning in Literature,* edited by Nicholas Karolides. White Plains, NY: Longman.

Moore, John Noell. 1997. *Interpreting Young Adult Literature: Literary Theory in the Secondary Classroom.* Portsmouth, NH: Boynton/Cook.

Rosenblatt, Louise. 1938. *Literature as Exploration*. New York: D. Appleton-Century Crofts, Inc.

## Resources on Writing as Learning Tool

Bertoff, Ann. 1981. *The Making of Meaning: Metaphors, Models and Maxims for Writing Teachers*. Portsmouth, NH: Boynton/Cook.

Britton, J. N. 1970. *Language and Learning*. London: Penguin.

Bruffee, Kenneth. 1984. "Collaborative Learning and the 'Conversation of Mankind.'" *College English* 46: 635–52.

Bruner, Jerome. 1973. *Beyond the Information Given: Studies in the Pyschology of Knowing*. New York: Norton.

Martin, Nancy. 1983. *Mostly About Writing: Selected Essays by Nancy Martin*. Portsmouth, NH: Boynton/Cook.

Mayher, John S., Nancy Lester, and Gordon M. Pradl. 1983. *Learning to Write/Writing to Learn*. Portsmouth, NH: Boynton/Cook.

Olson, D. R. 1977. "From Utterance to Text: the Bias of Speech in Thought and Action." *Harvard Educational Review* 47: 257–81.

## Works Cited

Andrews, Sharon. 1989. "Teaching as Inquiry: Contexts that Empower." Paper presented at the International Reading Conference, New Orleans, Louisiana, May 4. ERIC Document ED310085.

Apple, Michael. 1979. *Ideology and Curriculum*. London: Routledge and Kegan Paul.

Arhar, Joanne M., J. Howard Johnston, and Glenn C. Markle. 1992. "The Effects of Teaming on Students." In *Connecting the Curriculum through Interdisciplinary Instruction*, edited by J. Lounsbury, 23–35. Columbus, OH: National Middle School Association.

Auerbach, E. R., and D. Burgess. 1985. "The Hidden Curriculum of Survival ESL." *TESOL Quarterly* 19(3): 475–95.

Atkinson, J. W. 1964. *An Introduction to Motivation*. Princeton, NJ: Van Nostrand.

Bandura, A. 1986. *Social Foundations of Thought and Action*. Englewood Cliffs, NJ: Prentice Hall.

Berry, J. E., and J. Valentine. 1993. "The Organizational Structure of Effective Middle Schools." In *Middle School Research: Selected Studies, 1974–1993*, edited by D. B. Strahan. Columbus, OH: National Middle School Association.

Brophy, Jere. 1979. "Teacher Behavior and Student Learning." *Educational Leadership* 37: 33–38.

Christenson, Charlene Noelan-Kahuanui, and Jacquelin H. Carroll. 1995. "Teaching and Learning About Student Goal-Setting in a Fifth-Grade Classroom." *Language Arts* 72(1): 42–49.

Cornbleth, Catherine. 1978. *Inquiry Theory and Social Studies Curricular Problems in Planning for Thinking.* Paper presented at the Annual Meeting of the American Educational Research Association, Toronto, Ontario, March 27–31. ERIC Document ED152646.

Crowley, Paul. 1995. "Listening to What Readers Tell Us." *Voices from the Middle* 2(2): 3–12.

cummings, e. e. 1976. "in Just—." In *Tulips and Chimneys.* New York: Liveright.

Farrell, Edmund. 1966. "Listen My Children, and You Shall Read." *English Journal* 55(1): 39–45, 68.

Foster, Harold M. 1994. *Crossing Over: Whole Language for Secondary English Teachers.* New York: Harcourt Brace College Publishers.

Freire, Paulo. 1970. *Pedagogy of the Oppressed.* New York: Continuum.

———. 1985. *The Politics of Education.* South Hadley, MA: Bergin and Garvey.

Frost, Robert. 1939. "Mending Wall." In *The Complete Poems of Robert Frost.* New York: Henry Holt.

George, Paul S., and William M. Alexander. 1993. *The Exemplary Middle School,* 2d ed. New York: Harcourt, Brace, Jovanovich College Division.

Giroux, Henry. 1983. *Theory and Resistance in Education.* South Hadley, MA: Bergin and Garvey.

Goodman, Kenneth. 1986. *What's Whole in Whole Language.* Portsmouth, NH: Heinemann.

Hilke, V. E. 1990. *Cooperative Learning.* Bloomington, IN: Phi Delta Kappa.

Hillocks, George. 1986. *Research on Written Composition: New Directions for Teaching.* Urbana, IL: National Council of Teachers of English.

Imdieke, Sandra. 1992. *Characters in Time Travel Fiction as Historical Guides.* ERIC Document ED350601.

Kerewsky, W. 1988. "Middle School: The 'I' of the Storm." *International Middle School Journal* (Spring).

Kim, Eugene C., and Richard D. Kellough. 1995. *A Resource Guide for Secondary School Teaching: Planning for Competence.* 6th ed. Englewood Cliffs, NJ: Merrill.

Kneedler, P. 1985. "California Assesses Critical Thinking." In *Developing Minds,* edited by Arthur Costa. Alexandria, VA: Association for Supervision and Curriculum Development.

Kritt, David. 1993. "Authenticity, Reflection, and Self-Evaluation in Alternative Assessment." *Middle School Journal* 25(2): 43–45.

Labbo, Linda, James Hoffman, and Nancy Rosen. 1995. "Ways to Unintentionally Make Writing Difficult." *Language Arts* 72(3): 164–70.

Lounsbury, John H., ed. 1992. *Connecting the Curriculum Through Interdisciplinary Instruction*. Columbus, OH: National Middle School Association.

Maryland Task Force on Middle Years Learning. 1989. *What Matters in the Middle Grades?* Baltimore, MD: Maryland State Department of Education.

McDaniel, T. R. 1977. "Principles of Classroom Discipline: Toward a Pragmatic Synthesis." *The Clearinghouse* 51: 149–52.

Meyer, Carol. 1992. "What's the Difference Between 'Authentic' and 'Performance' Assessment?" *Educational Leadership* 49(8): 39–40.

Olzewski, Pamela, and Regina Montenaro. 1995. "Reading Metropolis: Increasing Multicultural Awareness Through Trade Books." Paper presented at Annual Conference of the Ohio Council of Teachers of English Language Arts, Worthington, Ohio, March 9–11.

Probst, Robert. 1988. *Response and Analysis*. Portsmouth, NH: Boynton/Cook.

Rosenshine, B., and R. Stevens. 1986. "Teaching Functions." In *Handbook of Research on Teaching*, 3rd ed., edited by M. Wittrock, 376–91. New York: Macmillan.

Rosenbery, Ann S., Beth Warren, and Faith E. Conant. 1992. *Appropriating Scientific Discourse: Findings for Language Minority Classrooms—Research Report #3*. National Center for Research on Cultural Diversity and Second Language Learning. ERIC Document ED352263.

Shor, Ira. Ed. 1987. *Freire for the Classroom: A Sourcebook for Liberatory Teaching*. Portsmouth, NH: Boynton/Cook.

Slavin, Robert. 1980. "Effects of Student Teams and Peer Tutoring on Academic Achievement and Time on Task." *Journal of Experimental Education* 48: 252–57.

———. 1983. *Cooperative Learning*. New York: Longman.

———. 1984. "Students Motivating Students to Excel: Cooperative Incentives, Cooperative Tasks, and Student Achievement." *Elementary School Journal* 85: 53–64.

———. 1990. "Achievement Effects of Ability Grouping in Secondary Schools: A Best-Evidence Synthesis." *Review of Educational Research* 60: 471–500.

Slavin, R. E., N. L. Karweil, and N. A. Madden. 1989. *Effective Programs for Students at Risk*. Boston: Allyn and Bacon.

Smith, Frank. 1971. *Understanding Reading: A Psycholinguistic Analysis of Reading and Learning to Read*, 3d ed. New York: Holt, Rinehart and Winston.

———. 1992. "Learning to Read: The Never-Ending Debate." *Phi Delta Kappan* 72(February): 432–41.

Sternberg, Robert. 1985. *Beyond IQ: A Triarchic Theory of Human Intelligence*. New York: Cambridge University Press.

Stover, Lois, with Rita Karr. 1990. "Glasnost in the Classroom." *English Journal* 79: 47–53.

Stover, Lois, Gloria Neubert, and James Lawlor. 1993. *Creating Interactive Environments in the Secondary School.* Washington, DC: National Educational Association.

Sudol, David, and Peg Sudol. 1995. "Yet Another Story: Writers' Workshop Revisited." *Language Arts* 72(3): 171–78.

Traugh, Cecelia E. 1974. "Evaluating Inquiry Procedures." *Social Studies* 65(5): 201–02.

Treu, Carol Evans. 1995. "Luring Readers Out of Hiding." *Voices from the Middle* 2(2): 29–40.

vanAllen, Lanny. 1994. "English Language Arts Teachers Embracing Change and Making a Difference for Middle School Students." Paper presented at the National Council of Teachers of English Conference, Portland, Oregon, March 9.

Walberg, H. J. 1990. "Productive Teaching and Instruction: Assessing the Knowledge Base." *Phi Delta Kappan* 71(6): 470–78.

Wiles, Jon, and Joseph Bondi. 1993. *The Essential Middle School,* 2d ed. New York: Macmillan.

Wright, Judith A. 1995. "Not Just Words on a Page: Kids, Parents, and Teachers Learning About Reading Together." *Voices from the Middle* 2(2): 21–28.

## Young Adult Titles Cited

Beake, Leslie. 1993. *Song of Be.* New York: Henry Holt.

Cole, Brock. 1987. *The Goats.* New York: Farrar, Straus, Giroux.

Cormier, Robert 1974. *The Chocolate War.* New York: Pantheon.

Crutcher, Chris. 1993. *Staying Fat for Sarah Byrnes.* New York: Greenwillow.

Danziger, Paula. 1974. *The Cat Ate My Gymsuit.* New York: Delacorte.

Filipovic, Zlata. 1994. *Zlata's Diary: A Child's Life in Sarajevo.* New York: Viking.

Frank, Anne. 1952. *The Diary of a Young Girl.* Translated by B. M. Mooyaart. New York: Doubleday.

George, Jean Craighead. 1993. *The Fire Bug Connection.* New York: HarperCollins.

Gilson, Jamie. 1980. *Do Bananas Chew Gum?* New York: William Morrow.

Hobbs, Will. 1991. *Downriver.* New York: Atheneum.

Hunt, Irene. 1964. *Across Five Aprils.* Grove River, IL: Follet.

Irwin, Hadley. 1985. *Abby, My Love.* New York: Macmillan.

Klein, Gerda W. 1957. *All but My Life.* New York: The Noonday Press.

Korman, Gordon. 1985. *Don't Care High.* New York: Scholastic.

Likhanov, Albert. 1983. *Shadows Across the Sun.* New York: Harper and Row.

Little, Jean. 1995. *His Banner Over Me.* New York: Viking.

Lunn, Janet. 1983. *The Root Cellar*. New York: Scribner's Young Readers.

Meyer, Caroline. 1993. *White Lilacs*. New York: Gulliver Books (Harcourt Brace).

Naylor, Phyllis Reynolds. 1995. *Alice the Brave*. New York: Atheneum.

Okimoto, Jean D. 1995. *Talent Night*. New York: Scholastic.

Paterson, Katherine. 1973. *Sign of the Chrysanthemum*. New York: Crowell.

———. 1977. *Bridge to Terabithia*. New York: Crowell.

———. 1978. *The Great Gilly Hopkins*. New York: Crowell.

———. 1980. *Jacob Have I Loved*. New York: Crowell.

———. 1981. *Gates of Excellence: On Reading and Writing Books for Children*. New York: Lodestar (Dutton).

———. 1988. *Park's Quest*. New York: Lodestar (Dutton).

Paulsen, Gary. 1987. *Hatchet*. New York: Bradbury.

Phibrick, Roderick. 1993. *Freak the Mighty*. New York: Scholastic.

Powell, Randy. 1995. *Dean Duffy*. New York: Farrar, Straus, Giroux.

Sebestyen, Ouida. 1968. *Words by Heart*. Boston: Little, Brown.

Westall, Robert. 1992. *Gulf*. London: Metheun Children's Books.

# Appendix A

## Survey Results of Middle School Students' Relative Levels of Interest in Concepts with Potential for Transdisciplinary Planning

339 total surveys analyzed.

| | | | | | |
|---|---|---|---|---|---|
| *Gender*: | 169 Females | =49.9% | *School*: | 55 #1 = | 16.2% |
| | 170 Males = | 50.1% | | 160 #2 = | 47.3% |
| *Grade*: | 104 6th = | 30.7% | | 41 #3 = | 12.1% |
| | 159 7th = | 46.9% | | 21 #4 = | 6.2% |
| | 76 8th = | 22.4% | | 62 #5 = | 18.3% |

Note:  * indicates a significant difference in *P* at the .05 level
     ** indicates a difference in *P* significant at the .01 level

| | Total Po. | Males | Females | |
|---|---|---|---|---|
| Concept | Mean | Mean | Mean | Sig. of P |
| 1. Courage | 3.210 | 3.17 | 3.25 | .532 |
| 2. Community | 2.487 | 2.65 | 2.33 | *.022 |
| 3. Communication | 2.880 | 3.04 | 2.74 | *.044 |
| 4. Expression | 2.896 | 3.23 | 2.59 | **.000 |
| 5. Patterns | 2.411 | 2.46 | 2.36 | .476 |
| 6. Change | 3.059 | 3.21 | 2.89 | *.022 |
| 7. Proof | 2.639 | 2.63 | 2.89 | .851 |
| 8. Time | 2.719 | 2.62 | 2.81 | .196 |
| 9. Structure | 2.774 | 2.62 | 2.81 | .235 |
| 10. Design | 3.425 | 3.55 | 3.31 | .126 |
| 11. Adaptation | 2.976 | 3.01 | 2.94 | .603 |

| Concept | Total Po. Mean | Males Mean | Females Mean | Sig. of P |
|---|---|---|---|---|
| 12. Survival | 3.982 | 3.84 | 4.16 | *.016 |
| 13. Trends | 3.158 | 3.43 | 2.89 | **.000 |
| 14. Exploration | 3.819 | 3.58 | 4.08 | **.001 |
| 15. Balance | 2.559 | 2.51 | 2.60 | .496 |
| 16. Extinction | 3.089 | 3.01 | 3.14 | .429 |
| 17. Cultures | 3.068 | 3.34 | 2.79 | **.000 |
| 18. Style | 3.425 | 3.66 | 3.19 | **.002 |
| 19. Conflict | 4.694 | 4.68 | 4.71 | .810 |
| 20. Truth | 3.195 | 3.39 | 3.00 | **.010 |
| 21. Beginnings | 2.688 | 2.72 | 2.65 | .629 |
| 22. Symbols | 2.846 | 2.79 | 2.88 | .547 |
| 23. Energy | 3.175 | 2.90 | 3.44 | **.001 |
| 24. Relationships | 3.469 | 3.89 | 3.04 | **.000 |
| 25. Forces | 3.097 | 2.68 | 3.52 | **.000 |
| 26. Progress | 2.719 | 2.71 | 2.74 | .811 |
| 27. Independence | 3.383 | 3.53 | 3.25 | .070 |
| 28. Honor | 3.358 | 3.40 | 3.31 | .543 |
| 29. Environments | 3.399 | 3.53 | 3.26 | .079 |
| 30. Immigration | 2.555 | 2.69 | 2.42 | .075 |
| 31. Origins | 2.769 | 2.71 | 2.82 | .440 |
| 32. War | 3.599 | 3.07 | 4.12 | **.001 |
| 33. Influences | 2.950 | 3.02 | 2.86 | .249 |
| 34. Confrontation | 3.054 | 2.98 | 3.11 | .411 |
| 35. Freedom | 3.714 | 3.80 | 3.61 | .202 |
| 36. Color | 3.215 | 3.38 | 3.04 | *.029 |
| 37. Space | 3.330 | 2.93 | 3.72 | **.000 |
| 38. Frontiers | 2.805 | 2.52 | 3.09 | **.000 |
| 39. Boundaries | 2.491 | 2.42 | 2.56 | .295 |
| 40. Beliefs | 3.032 | 3.27 | 2.79 | **.002 |
| 41. Justice | 3.230 | 3.36 | 3.17 | .211 |
| 42. Sources | 2.475 | 2.46 | 2.43 | .669 |
| 43. Rights | 3.307 | 3.39 | 3.21 | .269 |
| 44. Power | 3.769 | 3.55 | 3.99 | **.002 |
| 45. Cycles | 2.606 | 2.52 | 2.67 | .309 |
| 46. Behavior | 3.174 | 3.37 | 2.96 | **.005 |
| 47. Tradition | 3.130 | 3.40 | 2.87 | **.000 |
| 48. Homes | 3.025 | 3.22 | 2.84 | *.019 |
| 49. Overall interest | 3.450 | 3.40 | 3.49 | .541 |

## Survey Results—Top 15 Concepts Overall

Note: The # indicates an item appearing on the top ten list for both females and males. The @ indicates an item appearing on the top ten list for females. The ! indicates an item appearing on the top ten list for males.

|  | Mean Score | Females | Males | Sig. of P |
|---|---|---|---|---|
| 1. Conflict # | 4.694 | 4.68 | 4.71 | .810 |
| 2. Survival # | 3.982 | 3.84 | 4.16 | *.016 |
| 3. Exploration # | 3.819 | 3.58 | 4.08 | **.001 |
| 4. Power # | 3.769 | 3.55 | 3.99 | **.002 |
| 5. Freedom # | 3.714 | 3.80 | 3.61 | .202 |
| 6. War ! | 3.599 | 3.07 | 4.12 | **.000 |
| 7. Relationships @ | 3.469 | 3.89 | 3.04 | **.000 |
| 8. Design ! | 3.425 | 3.55 | 3.31 | .126 |
| 9. Style @ | 3.425 | 3.66 | 3.19 | **.002 |
| 10. Environments @ | 3.399 | 3.53 | 3.26 | .079 |
| 11. Independence @ | 3.383 | 3.53 | 3.25 | .070 |
| 12. Honor ! | 3.358 | 3.40 | 3.31 | .543 |
| 13. Space ! | 3.330 | 2.93 | 3.72 | **.000 |
| 14. Rights | 3.307 | 3.39 | 3.21 | .269 |
| 15. Courage | 3.210 | 3.17 | 3.25 | .532 |

Behavior and traditions appeared on the top ten list as rated by females; energy appeared on the top ten list as rated by males.

## Five Concepts of Least Interest Overall

Note: The # indicates items ranked of very low interest by both females and males.

|  | Mean Score | Females | Males | Sig. of P |
|---|---|---|---|---|
| 1. Balance | 2.559 | 2.51 | 2.60 | .496 |
| 2. Immigration | 2.555 | 2.69 | 3.26 | .079 |
| 3. Boundaries # | 2.491 | 2.42 | 2.56 | .295 |
| 4. Sources | 2.475 | 2.49 | 2.43 | .669 |
| 5. Patterns # | 2.411 | 2.46 | 2.36 | .476 |

Additionally, frontiers, justice, and cycles were ranked in the bottom five on the female list; males rated community among their five least favorite concepts, and balance was not among the bottom five concepts as rated by males.

## Top Ten Concepts as Ranked by Females

Note: The # indicates concepts rated of high interest by females which were not in the top ten concepts overall; the @ indicates items rated highly by females which were not in the top ten list as ranked by males.

| Concept | Female Mean | Male Mean | Sig. of P |
|---|---|---|---|
| 1. Conflict | 4.68 | 4.71 | .810 |
| 2. Relationships @ | 3.89 | 3.04 | **.000 |
| 3. Survival | 3.84 | 4.16 | *.016 |
| 4. Freedom | 3.80 | 3.61 | .202 |
| 5. Style @ | 3.66 | 3.19 | **.002 |
| 6. Exploration | 3.58 | 4.08 | **.001 |
| 7. Power | 3.55 | 3.99 | **.002 |
| 8. Traditions #, @ | 3.40 | 2.87 | **.000 |
| 9. Independence #, @ | 3.53 | 3.25 | .070 |
| 10. Environments @ | 3.53 | 3.26 | .079 |
| 11. Behavior #, @ | 3.37 | 2.96 | **.005 |

## Top Ten Concepts as Ranked by Males

Note: # indicates concepts rated of high interest by males which were not in the top ten concepts overall; @ indicates items rated highly by males which were not in the top ten list as ranked by females.

| Concept | Male Mean | Female Mean | Sig. of P |
|---|---|---|---|
| 1. Conflict | 4.71 | 4.68 | .810 |
| 2. Survival | 4.16 | 3.84 | *.016 |
| 3. War @ | 4.12 | 3.07 | **.001 |
| 4. Exploration | 4.08 | 3.58 | **.001 |
| 5. Power | 3.99 | 3.55 | **.002 |
| 6. Space #, @ | 3.72 | 2.93 | **.000 |
| 7. Freedom | 3.61 | 3.80 | .202 |
| 8. Forces #, @ | 3.52 | 2.68 | **.000 |
| 9. Energy #, @ | 3.44 | 2.90 | **.001 |
| 10. Honor #, @ | 3.31 | 3.40 | .543 |
| 11. Design @ | 3.31 | 3.55 | .126 |

## Survey Results—School

There were several significant differences among items as analyzed by school. For the purposes of this text, these results have not been reported because it is difficult to generalize about the interest level in a concept at a school level from a sample size of only twenty-two students drawn from a population of over five hundred. The schools do, however, serve quite different populations. School #1 serves students from a suburban community of professionals with a high income level mixed with an increasing number of students whose parents have recently immigrated to the United States from various Slavic countries. School #2 serves a widely diverse population of suburban students who vary in their cultural background and significantly differ in their socioeconomic status. School #3 serves a population of 97 percent urban, African American students of very diverse income levels. School #4 serves a population from an urban, working-class neighborhood that is divided fairly evenly between Caucasian and African American students. School #5 serves a rural farming community with many recent transfers from an urban environment as well as from abroad—whose students are diverse in their cultural background and economic status. Eventually, with more data, it will be interesting to see whether or not these diverse populations do, in fact, have significantly different levels of interest in certain concepts because of the diverse nature of their needs and concerns.

## Analysis of Results

From the narrative responses to the open-ended questions it is apparent that students do not necessarily recognize interdisciplinary unit structures. For instance, while some students said they had studied the Canadian wilderness and the Appalachian Trail in interdisciplinary fashion, others thought that reading *Tom Sawyer* counted as an interdisciplinary experience—which it could be, but was not, given their descriptions of their experiences. Uniformly, those students who said they had experienced interdisciplinary units identified the English language arts classroom as the place where interdisciplinary study happened. Very few students—twenty-three—identified learning experiences in which teams of teachers actually worked together to help them explore concepts from multiple perspectives. It seems that if we really want students to engage in true inquiry in interdisciplinary ways, we will have to help them recognize that they are, in fact, learning content that is traditionally associated with specific disciplines, and we will have to be explicit about how the skills we teach cross content-area boundaries. And we will have to ensure that when we work together to plan such units students are aware of the process of cooperation in which we ourselves are engaged so that they perceive us as models of teaming.

The comments from the survey were interesting. One young man thought all of the concepts listed on the survey were "boring" and "irrelevant." He then wrote that I needed to talk about things that were really important and happening in his life. He suggested concepts such as racial tension, poverty, AIDS, and pollution in the Chesapeake Bay. He had no way of generalizing these specifics under the heading of "conflict" or seeing how "environments" would also serve as an umbrella concept. Many other students gave similar suggestions. Perhaps their responses are simply reflective of the fairly typical adolescent thinking skill level, one that hovers between concrete operational and formal operational. Many students wrote notes on the survey about concepts like color or boundaries, saying they did not "get" what I meant and could not see how they could study such a concept from more than one perspective. Color, for instance, they could only interpret from an artist's point of view, while boundaries seemed to them like a math concept. Those comments suggest that as teachers we can do a better job of explaining the connections among concepts, skills, and knowledge across traditional content-area boundaries.

It seems worth noting that males and females do have significantly different interests at the middle school level. Of the top fifteen concepts, male and female scores for seven items were significantly different; there were two items, behavior and traditions, in the top ten list for females that did not make it into the male top ten, nor did they make it into the overall top fifteen, and energy ranked in the top ten items for the males but not for females. Some items, such as war, design, honor, space, relationships, style, environments, and independence made it into the top ten list overall because of the strong ratings received from members of one sex or the other. War, for instance, only received a mean score of 3.07 from the female responders, while the mean score for the males was a 4.12. Clearly, then, teachers will have to work hard to find texts for units centered on such concepts that will appeal to both males and females and will have to be explicit about the ways in which various concepts connect to the interests of their male and female students. Perhaps choosing a "war" book such as Choi's *The Year of Impossible Good-byes*, a novel about the Korean war with a female protagonist, will help students begin to discover similarities of interest and perspective that cross gender lines.

# Appendix B

# Texts for Young Adults
# Annotated by Concept

## Courage

**Freedman, Russell. 1993.** *Eleanor Roosevelt: A Life of Discovery.* **New York: Clarion.**

Biography of Eleanor Roosevelt demonstrating her integrity and the courage she displayed throughout her life as both a public personage and private person.

**Volavkova, Hana, ed. 1993.** *I Never Saw Another Butterfly: Children's Drawings and Poems from Terezin Concentration Camp, 1942–1944.* **New York: Schocken.**

Collection of poems written by children interned in concentration camps during World War II.

**Taylor, Theodore. 1969.** *The Cay.* **New York: Doubleday.**

Eleven-year-old Philip and seventy-year-old Timothy spend three months together on a tiny cay, surviving only because they are able to forget their differences and support each other through their ordeal. Sequel—*Timothy of the Cay.* 1993. New York: Avon.

## Community

**Lasky, Kathryn. 1983.** *Beyond the Divide.* **New York: Macmillan.**

Shunned by their Amish community, Meribah and her father join a wagon train and head west.

**Lee, Harper. 1960.** *To Kill a Mockingbird.* **New York: Lippincott.**

Atticus Finch defies community standards to defend a Black man against charges brought by a White man, and teaches his children about the meaning of honor in the process.

**Oughton, Jerrie. 1995.** *Music from a Place Called Half Moon.* **Boston: Houghton Mifflin.**

It is the 1950s. When thirteen-year-old Edie Jo's father announces that the vacation Bible school should be open to Blacks, the social fabric of the small Appalachian community is disturbed.

**Taylor, Mildred. 1976.** *Roll of Thunder, Hear My Cry.* **New York: Dial.**

Cassie Logan and her family experience hardship and joy as they farm their land during the Depression, trying to maintain their integrity as African Americans in a White man's world.

## Power

**Carmody, Isobelle. 1993.** *The Gathering.* **New York: Dial.**

Nathaniel begins to explore the past history of his new town, Cheshunt, and stumbles onto evil and corrupted power, which he and a group of friends attempt to combat.

**Cormier, Robert. 1974.** *The Chocolate War.* **New York: Pantheon.**

Archie embodies the ways in which power can seduce in this tale of how the Vigils, under his command, control Trinity High School by using both psychological and physical force—until Jerry Renault decides to disturb their universe.

**Rapp, Adam. 1994.** *Missing the Piano.* **New York: Viking.**

When Mike has to attend St. Matthew's Military Academy, he learns about bullying and bigotry and experiences a violence he's never known before.

## Communication

**Cleary, Beverly. 1983.** *Dear Mr. Henshaw.* **New York: William Morrow Junior Books.**

Leigh Botts writes to Mr. Henshaw as a way to figure out how to cope with his parents' divorce, a lunch-box thief, and other tribulations of sixth grade.

**Fox, Paula. 1995.** *The Eagle Kite.* **New York: Orchard (Richard Jackson).**

When Liam, a freshman, learns his father is dying of AIDS, he has a vivid memory of seeing his father on a beach embracing another man, and he begins to untangle the web of family secrets that has resulted in so much grief.

**Marsden, John. 1994.** *Letters from the Inside.* **Boston: Houghton Mifflin.**

Tracy and Mandy are pen pals who reveal a little more of themselves and their terrible problems each time they write a letter, but do they ever really get to know each other completely?

# Expression

**Brooks, Bruce. 1989.** *Celine.* **New York: Farrar, Straus, Giroux.**

Celine tries to "show a little maturity" as her father asks of her before he takes off for two months, but she is having trouble doing so because of problems with her very young stepmother, her friend's father, her school paper on *Catcher in the Rye*, and her latest painting, "Test Patterns."

**Paterson, Katherine. 1995.** *Come Sing, Jimmy Jo.* **New York: Puffin (Frederick Warne).**

Jimmy has to figure out how to be true to his musical gifts while being true to his family at the same time.

**Voigt, Cynthia. 1992.** *Orfe.* **New York: Scholastic.**

Loosely based on the myth of Orpheus, Voigt's unusual love story describes the darker side of the music industry and how young musicians often have more to contend with than they can bear.

# Patterns

**Annixter, Paul. 1950.** *Swiftwater.* **New York: A. A. Wyn.**

Bucky Calloway feels a kinship and love for the wild geese who return every year to their Maine farm, and he decides to establish a wild game preserve for them.

**Hentoff, Nat. 1965.** *Jazz Country.* **New York: HarperCollins.**

The patterns of music and of life are explored in this story of a white boy trying to break into the black world of jazz.

**Naylor, Phyllis Reynolds. 1982.** *A String of Chances.* **New York: Atheneum.**

Sixteen-year-old Evie begins to question the cycle of life and death when she leaves the familiarity of her home and church to help her cousin care for her newborn, who dies suddenly, upsetting the balance of reality as Evie has known it.

**Pringle, Laurence. 1990.** *Global Warming: Assessing the Greenhouse Effect.* **Berkeley, CA: Arcade.**

Pringle provides a useful discussion of the changes in global warming patterns and raises questions central to determining their effect.

# Change

**Johnston, Julie. 1994.** *Adam and Eve and Pinch Me.* **Boston: Little, Brown.**

Sara Moore, a fifteen-year-old foster child, uses the computer keys "delete, move, change," to try to control her world, but finally, when she finds herself with the Huddlestons, she finds that she may no longer want to delete, move, or change her life.

**Kerr, M. E. 1986.** *Night Kites.* **New York: HarperCollins.**

During his senior year, Erik has to cope with the fact of his brother's AIDS, deciding whether to continue as a "day kite," a part of the "in crowd," or whether to become a "night kite," unafraid of flying alone and being different.

**Marcus, Leonard S., ed. 1994.** *Lifelines: A Poetry Anthology Patterned on the Stages of Life.* **New York: Dutton Children's Books.**

In four sections, "Small Traveler," "I Am Old Enough," "On Such a Hill," and "In the End We Are All Light," this poetry volume gives voice to the human experience from birth to death.

**Paterson, Katherine. 1977.** *Bridge to Terabithia.* **New York: Crowell.**

When Leslie beats Jess to become the fastest runner in the fifth grade, Jess's hopes for the year are dashed, but as he and Leslie begin to create a special friendship, to build their own special kingdom, Jess begins to gain self-esteem and is able, ultimately, to deal with the most final change—death.

**Voigt, Cynthia. 1981.** *Homecoming*. **New York: Atheneum.**

After her mother abandons Dicey and her younger siblings in a parking lot, Dicey takes care of them, using her strength and intelligence to get the family to their grandmother's home, and then, as Dicey has to accept a new set of circumstances, both she and her grandmother have to change.

# Proof

**Davis, Jenny. 1988.** *Sex Education*. **New York: Orchard.**

For their high school biology class Livvie and David have to care for someone; in the process, they learn just how difficult and risky caring for another can be.

**Lasky, Kathryn. 1994.** *Beyond the Burning Time*. **New York: Blue Sky Press (Scholastic).**

Twelve-year-old Mary and her mother struggle to run the family farm just outside Salem, while the entire community struggles to determine whether the town has been infested with witches.

**Cushman, Karen. 1995.** *The Midwife's Apprentice*. **New York: Clarion.**

Thirteen-year-old Alyce is found in a dungheap by a midwife in the 14th century. She becomes the older woman's apprentice, but seems to lack the skill needed to follow in her footsteps; it is not until she leaves her mentor that she finds the proof of her own abilities she needs to be successful.

# Time

**Ferris, Jean. 1994.** *Signs of Life*. **New York: Farrar, Straus, Giroux.**

After her twin, "the good daughter," is killed by a drunken driver, Hannah has to adapt to life on her own, a process enhanced through the vivid dreams and visions/flashbacks in time caused by her visit to the Lascaux caves of France and through her short-lived but intense romance with a Romany circus performer.

**L'Engle, Madeleine. 1962.** *A Wrinkle in Time.* **New York: Farrar, Straus, Giroux.**

Meg, with the help of three benign witches, must "tesseract," or travel through wrinkles in time, to save her father and younger brother from the ominous "It."

**Service, Pamela. 1989.** *Vision Quest.* **New York: Atheneum.**

Kate finds an ancient shaman's artifact that sends her visions from times past; eventually, she must travel back in time to help the Indians who peopled the site of her Nevada town, learning something about what it means to be human no matter where or when you live.

**Naylor, Phyllis Reynolds. 1980.** *Shadows on the Wall* **(York Trilogy Vol. I). 1981.** *Faces in the Water* **(York Trilogy Vol. II). 1981.** *Footprints at the Window* **(York Trilogy Vol. III). New York: Atheneum.**

As Dan travels through time, to the York of Roman days and to York during the Black Plague years, he becomes more able to cope with the realities of his uncertain present—a present dominated by the inability of medical science to tell him and his father whether they carry the gene for the totally disabling Huntington's Disease.

# Structure

**Duffy, Betsy. 1994.** *Coaster.* **New York: Viking.**

Twelve-year-old Hart tries to maintain his tenuous links with his roller-coaster-loving father by building one of his own in the woods behind his mother's house.

**Macauley, David. 1988.** *The Way Things Work: From Levers to Lasers, Cars to Computers—A Visual Guide to the World of Machines.* **Boston: Houghton Mifflin.**

Macauley's title is an accurate description of the delights of this text, which provides insights into the structure of machines of all sorts.

**Zindel, Paul. 1969.** *The Pigman.* **New York: HarperCollins.**

Lorraine and John take turns telling the story of their relationship with each other and Mr. Pignati in this well-structured exploration of how their encounters with him change their lives forever.

# Design

**Howker, Janni. 1995.** *The Topiary Garden.* **New York: Orchard.**

Reluctantly spending a weekend with her father and brother at a motorcycle race, Liz finds refuge in the lovely design of the topiary garden of the house on whose grounds the race is being held. There she meets elderly Sally Beck, who tells Liz the story of her youth, during which she pretended to be a boy so that she could learn to cut and shape the plants.

**Lowry, Lois. 1993.** *The Giver.* **Boston: Houghton Mifflin.**

When Jonas is twelve, he receives his lifetime assignment to be the "receiver of memories," and he begins to learn the terrible truths about the ways in which his society is designed and operated.

**Yep, Laurence. 1975.** *Dragon Wings.* **New York: HarperCollins.**

With this fictionalized account of a Chinese immigrant to California who, in 1909, designed a flying machine that stayed airborne for twenty minutes, Yep shows his readers that the thousands of Chinese who came to America at the turn of the century were not merely statistics, but were real people, with real hopes and dreams and visions of a better future.

# Adaptation

**Conrad, Pam. 1995.** *Our House: Stories of Levittown.* **New York: Scholastic.**

Children of Levittown chronicle what it was like to grow up in the town during each decade from the 1940s to the 1990s, showing how the suburb has adapted to changes over time against a backdrop of American history.

**Crompton, Anne Eliot. 1982.** *The Sorcerer.* **Sag Harbor, NY: Second Chance.**

In this historical novel, Lefthand, an Indian boy, injured by a bear, cannot hunt—a serious situation because that is what the men of the tribe do; however, he eventually wins the respect of his people by developing his artistic skill and using them in service to their hunting rituals.

**McNair, Joseph. 1989.** *Commander Coatrack Returns.* **Boston: Houghton Mifflin.**

Lisa has to adapt to her parents' decision to enroll younger brother Cody in a special school, to friend Van's increasingly militant feminism, to the bullying of Jimmy, and to her newfound friendship with Robert, but are the strategies she is using to cope ultimately maladaptive instead of truly useful?

**Reuter, Bjarne. 1994.** *The Boys from St. Petri.* **Translated by Anthea Bell. New York: Dutton.**

A group of teenage boys take on increasingly dangerous resistance missions rather than adapt to the new way of life that occupying German soliders attempt to impose on them in their native Denmark during World War II.

**Salisbury, Graham. 1994.** *Under the Blood-Red Sun.* **New York: Delacorte.**

When both his father and grandfather are interned after the bombing of Pearl Harbor, Tomi, a Hawaiian teen, has to become the man of his Japanese American family.


# Survival

The following titles are all annotated in Chapter 4 under the subheading "Tales of Physical Survival." In addition, fourteen other titles, reflecting survival in difficult emotional contexts, are discussed.

**Cole, Brock. 1987.** *The Goats.* **New York: Farrar, Straus, Giroux.**

**Hobbs, Will. 1991.** *Downriver.* **New York: Atheneum.**

**Klein, Gerda Weissman. 1995.** *All but My Life.* **New York: Hill and Wang (Farrar, Straus, Giroux).**

**Paulsen, Gary. 1987.** *Hatchet.* **New York: Bradbury.**

**Sebestyen, Ouida. 1988.** *The Girl in the Box.* **Boston: Joy Street Books (Little, Brown).**

**Taylor, Theodore. 1994.** *Sweet Friday Island.* **New York: Harcourt Brace.**

**Wartski, Maureen Crane. 1980.** *A Boat to Nowhere.* **New York: Signet.**

# Trends

**Ashabranner, Brent. 1987.** *Into a Strange Land: Unaccompanied Refugee Youth in America.* **New York: Dodd, Mead.**

Ashabranner tells the stories of recent teenage immigrants to the United States, describing how and why they have come to this country, and their struggles to survive here on their own.

**Bode, Janet. 1990.** *The Voices of Rape.* **New York: Franklin Watts.**

One out of every four women experiences sexual intercourse for the first time through rape, and Bode, a survivor of rape, presents interviews with the various people involved in and affected by the brutal act of rape.

**Dickinson, Peter. 1989.** *Eva.* **New York: Delacorte.**

As scientists continue to discover new technologies, this story of how Eva's brain and memory patterns are transplanted into the body of Kelly, a chimpanzee, becomes less improbable, and Dickinson explores the implications of such discoveries.

**Peck, Richard. 1976.** *Are You in the House Alone?* **New York: Viking.**

A high school girl is harassed and eventually raped by a classmate, but her family and peers have trouble viewing her as the victim, and her attacker goes free.

# Exploration

**Graham, Robin Lee, and Derek L. T. Gill. 1972.** *Dove.* **New York: Harper and Row.**

At sixteen, Graham set out to circle the globe alone, by sailboat; *Dove* is the narrative account of his explorations of both the sea, other countries, and his own psyche.

**Jacobs, Francine. 1992.** *The Tainos: The People Who Welcomed Columbus.* **New York: Putnam.**

Jacobs describes the Tainos, inhabitants of the Caribbean who welcomed Columbus, and how the Spaniards exploration of their environment resulted eventually in their extinction.

**LeGuin, Ursula. 1969.** *The Left-Hand of Darkness.* **New York: Ace.**

Mixing science fiction and fantasy, LeGuin explores gender restrictions by presenting a world in which the people are neither male nor female.

**Paulsen, Gary. 1994. *The Car*. New York: Harcourt Brace.**

When fourteen-year-old Terry Anders is abandoned by his parents, he assembles a car kit and heads west to Oregon, picking up a forty-five-year-old wandering Vietnam vet, Waylon Jackson, who guides his exploration of the countryside and of what it means to engage in the learning process.

# Balance

**Carter, Alden. 1990. *RoboDad*. New York: G. P. Putnam. (Released by Scholastic, 1994, as *Dancing on Dark Water*.)**

Shar and her dad used to be best buddies, but that was before an artery ruptured in Dad's head, leaving him more like a robot than a real person, and now Shar is doing her best to bring her dad back and make her family whole again.

**Blume, Judy. 1976. *Tiger Eyes*. New York: Bradbury.**

Davey and her mother both struggle to restore balance to their lives after Davey's father is killed during a robbery and they leave the east coast for a very different life in Los Alamos.

**Hall, Barbara. 1990. *Dixie Storms*. New York: Harcourt Brace Jovanovich.**

When Dutch is fifteen, her cousin comes to visit for the summer, upsetting the delicate balance Dutch's unusual family has attempted to preserve in their lives.

**Isaacson, Philip. 1988. *Round Buildings, Square Buildings, and Buildings That Wriggle Like a Fish*. New York: Alfred Knopf.**

Through photography, Isaacson shows the kinds of balance and effects on viewers' moods and feelings that architects strive to achieve when designing buildings of all sorts.

# Justice

**Armstrong, William. 1969. *Sounder*. New York: HarperCollins.**

When a sharecropper is arrested for stealing a ham and sent away, his son follows the chain gangs searching for his father.

**Cooney, Carolyn. 1994. *Driver's Ed*. New York: Delacorte.**

Two high school students steal a stop sign and have to live with the horrible consequences of their action, learning about justice and mercy and redemptive power of love in the process.

**Naylor, Phyllis Reynolds. 1991. *Shiloh*. New York: Atheneum.**

Eleven-year-old Marty tries to define justice and fairness when he befriends a hound dog, Shiloh, whose owner mistreats it.

**Temple, Frances. 1992. *A Taste of Salt: A Modern History of Haiti*. New York: Richard Jackson (Orchard).**

Djo, young man of the streets, hovers near death in a Haitian hospital, recovering from the terrorist bombing that killed his friends. Jeremie, a convent girl, has been sent by Aristide to record Djo's story. Their voices intertwine, telling their own stories and that of a Haiti struggling, under Aristide, towards democratic reform.

## Extinction

**Fletcher, Susan. 1994. *Flight of the Dragon Kyn*. New York: Jean Karl (Atheneum).**

The king wants Kara, fifteen, to help him destroy the dragons who once saved her life by using her special powers in this fantasy novel set in the same world as that of *Dragon's Milk*.

**Klass, David. 1994. *California Blue*. New York: Scholastic.**

When John discovers a new species of butterfly and notifies the environmental lobbyists, his town turns against him. Not only does he have to cope with their anger, he has to cope with the reality of his father's newly diagnosed cancer as well as his father's disappointment in his choices.

**O'Brien, Robert. 1975. *Z for Zachariah*. New York: Atheneum.**

Ann Burden is, at first, alone, a survivor of a nuclear holocaust, but she eventually leaves the comparative safety of "Hidden Valley," searching for companions with whom she can build a new social order.

## Cultures

**Crew, Linda. 1989. *Children of the River*. New York: Delacorte.**

Sundara, a refugee from Cambodia, tries to fit into a new life in an Oregon high school, but has to figure out how to balance her loyalty to her family and culture with her growing loyalty to her American boyfriend.

**Soto, Gary. 1989.** *Baseball in April.* **New York: Harcourt, Brace, Jovanovich.**

This collection of stories details the daily life of Hispanic American young people growing up in California.

**Thomas, Joyce Carol. 1982.** *Marked by Fire.* **New York: Avon.**

Abby achieves recognition as a healer and leader of her community.

# Style

**Danes, Meredith. 1988.** *Francie and the Boys.* **New York: Dell.**

Francie, quiet and dreamy, turns out to have the talent needed to be selected as one of the six girls to act in a play at a London boys' school, but she has to find her own style as the rehearsal schedule unfolds.

**Lester, Julius. 1995.** *Othello: A Novel.* **New York: Scholastic.**

Lester's prose blends wonderfully with Shakespeare's poetry in this version of the classic, in which Iago, Desdemona, and Othello share a friendship born in their native Africa.

**Trevino, Elizabeth de. 1965.** *I, Juan de Pareja.* **New York: Farrar, Straus, Giroux.**

Juan de Pareja was the servant of Spanish painter Velazquez; as he tells his story, the reader learns about the variations in color, light, and style among Rubens, Murillo, Juan's master, and, ultimately, Juan himself.

**Thompson, Julian. 1983.** *The Grounding of Group Six.* **New York: Avon.**

Thompson's breezy style serves him well as he unfolds this tale of five sixteen-year-olds who band together to survive when they learn that their teacher at an exclusive school is really a murderer for hire.

# Conflict

These titles, as well as several others, are annotated in Chapter 4, "Conflict and Confrontation."

**Hinojosa, Maria. 1995.** *Crews: Gang Members Talk to Maria Hinojosa.* **New York: Harcourt Brace.**

**Lee, Marie. 1994.** *Saying Goodbye.* **Boston: Houghton Mifflin.**

**Wolff, Virginia Euwer. 1993.** *Make Lemonade.* **New York: Scholastic.**

## Truth

**Avi. 1991.** *Nothing but the Truth: A Documentary Novel.* **New York: Orchard.**

Philip Malloy, track star, hums during the "Star Spangled Banner," earning him a trip to the office. Events take a dramatic turn, and Philip ends up suspended. Through a montage of memos, phone conversation transcripts, letters, newspaper articles, and journals, the readers have to piece together the truth of what happened and of its implications for issues of justice and human rights.

**Fine, Anne. 1988.** *Alias Madame Doubtfire.* **Boston: Houghton Mifflin.**

Who is Madame Doubtfire, and how can she help the father of Natalie, Christopher, and Lydia prove to their mother that he deserves to be a significant part of their lives?

**Houston, Jeanne Wakatsuki, and James D. Houston. 1973.** *Farewell to Manzanar.* **Boston: Houghton Mifflin.**

Jeanne Wakatsuki and her family were part of the more than 100,000 people of Japanese ancestry ordered into West Coast detention camps when the U.S. entered World War II; their three-year ordeal left their family shattered and left a legacy of low self-esteem that took years to erase.

**Miller, Frances. 1984.** *The Truth Trap.* **New York: Ballantine/Fawcett.**

Matt, aged fifteen, is accused of a murder he did not commit, and he learns a great deal about his personal relationships in the effort to clear his name.

**Murphy, Jim. 1995.** *The Great Fire.* **New York: Scholastic.**

Weaving together personal accounts of survivors of Chicago's great fire with carefully researched historical detail, combined with maps that show the inexorable spread of the blaze though the city, Murphy sheds new light on this event in a way that prompts the reader to ponder how the "truth" of any piece of history can ever be unquestionably accepted.

**Stowe, Rebecca. 1992.** *Not the End of the World.* **New York: Pantheon.**

When the novel opens, Maggie's grandmother is telling her friends that Maggie is crazy, but is there some truth to what seems to be just a joke?

# Beginnings

**Cooney, Caroline. 1991.** *The Party's Over.* **New York: Scholastic.**

When Hallie, prom queen and captain of the cheerleaders, is the only one of her crowd not to go away to college, she has to figure out what direction her life will take instead.

**Rodowsky, Colby. 1985.** *Julie's Daughter.* **New York: Farrar, Straus, Giroux.**

Julie and seventeen-year-old daughter Slug, whom Julie abandoned at birth, begin a new relationship while taking care of Harper Teggs, a dying artist; the story unfolds as the three characters alternate first-person narrative accounts of their experiences.

**Spinelli, Jerry. 1985.** *Night of the Whale.* **Boston: Little, Brown.**

Moose and his friends contemplate their future while at the beach for Senior Week, having fun and then helping to take care of beached and dying whales.

# Symbols

**Cormier, Robert. 1982.** *I Am the Cheese.* **New York: Knopf.**

Adam has been institutionalized as a result of government corruption and organized crime.

**Voigt, Cynthia. 1982.** *A Solitary Blue.* **New York: Atheneum.**

Jeff is like the solitary blue heron that he watches on his island retreat, but with his father's help, his pain, caused by his mother's continual betrayal of him, finally begins to ease.

**Walsh, Jill Peyton. 1987.** *Torch.* **New York: Viking Kestral.**

When Dio and Cal go to ask the old man's permission to marry, he tells them he is dying and commands them to become the "Guardian of the Torch," which they then bear with them throughout a remarkable journey in search of the Games and of the secrets of the past.

# Energy

**Fine, Ann. 1989.** *My War with Goggle Eyes.* **Boston: Little, Brown.**

Kitty didn't always like her stepdad, especially because he had rather different views on almost everything, including nuclear power.

**Gale, Robert Peter, and Thomas Hauser. 1988.** *Final Warning: The Legacy of Chernobyl.* **New York: Warner.**

Gale traveled to the Soviet Union during 1987 and 1988 to provide expert advice on radiation sickness and this book is his memoir of those experiences combined with a discussion of the consequences of nuclear technology in today's society.

**Hesse, Karen. 1994.** *Phoenix Rising.* **New York: Holt.**

Nyle lives with her grandmother on a Vermont sheep farm. They lead a fairly peaceful existence, until an accident at the nearby nuclear power plant changes their lives by forcing them to wear protective masks and to worry about contaminated food, and by leading Ezra, dying of radiation sickness, and his mother to take refuge with them.

**Lukas, Cynthia. 1983.** *Center Stage Summer.* **Ballston Lake, NY: Square One.**

Johanna's rebellious sister Dana gets her involved in a No Nukes movement against the Arkansas Weller nuclear power plant, for which Byron, Inc., makes equipment; unfortunately, it is from Byron, Inc., that Johanna has received a scholarship to study drama.

# Relationships

**Hamilton, Virginia. 1987.** *A White Romance.* **New York: Putnam.**

Talley and Didi form a friendship that crosses racial boundaries based on their love of running, but Talley's beliefs about both friendship and love are challenged when she begins to think that her boyfriend is supplying the drugs that are causing Didi's boyfriend's increasing dependency.

**Janeczko, Paul, ed. 1984.** *Strings: A Gathering of Family Poems.* **New York: Bradbury.**

These poems about grandparents, wives, children, siblings, and cousins are both funny and poignant.

**Mazer, Norma Fox. 1987.** *After the Rain.* **New York: William Morrow.**

Although Rachel hasn't cared much for her grumpy grandfather, when she learns he has terminal cancer, she begins talking with him, and ultimately realizes that she does, indeed, love him.

**Peck, Richard. 1985.** *Remembering the Good Times.* **New York: Delacorte.**

Buck and Kate and Trav have been great friends, in spite of the great differences in their backgrounds, but Buck and Kate can't keep Travis from disaster, and they are left "remembering the good times."

**Voigt, Cynthia. 1986.** *Izzy, Willy Nilly.* **New York: Atheneum.**

Izzy, at fifteen, is pretty and popular, but when she loses her leg in a drunk-driving accident she is forced to rethink her friendships and her values.

# Forces

**Carter, Alden. 1994.** *Dogwolf.* **New York: Scholastic.**

Pete LaSavage understands the anguish of the "dogwolf," howling to be free and wanting to be either dog or wolf, just as Pete longs to be either Chippewa or White, and during a summer of violent forest fires, Pete struggles with the turmoil that both surrounds him and eats at him from within.

**Cooper, Susan. 1973.** *The Dark is Rising.* **New York: Macmillan.**

On his eleventh birthday, Will Stanton discovers he is one of the "Old Ones," a group of immortals who have fought throughout the ages against the forces of evil. Will must learn to use his magic quickly because the Dark is rising in preparation for one final battle with the Light.

**Westall, Robert. 1988.** *Urn Burial.* **New York: Greenwillow.**

Seventeen-year-old Ralph decides to open the coffin of what turns out to have been an alien. Finding some equipment with which he experiments, he thereby sets the stage for some frightening confrontations with other aliens.

# Progress

**Brooks, Bruce. 1984.** *The Moves Make the Man.* **New York: HarperCollins.**

Thirteen-year-old Jerome narrates Bix's story, but it turns out to be as much a tale of his own maturing process as it is about Bix's difficult life.

**Johnson, Angela. 1995.** *Humming Whispers.* **New York: Richard Jackson (Orchard).**

Sophie fears she will end up like her sister, Nicole, who is schizophrenic, but with the help of Nicole and an elderly neighbor, Miss Onyx, Sophie is able to face her fear and develop her talents as a dancer.

**Lipsyte, Robert. 1977.** *One Fat Summer.* **New York: HarperCollins.**

Bobby Marks, overweight and fourteen, is feeling sorry for himself, but he embarks on a quest for self-respect, which he gains through his encounters with a number of different people who play a significant part in his life.

# Independence

**Cushman, Karen. 1994.** *Catherine, Called Birdie.* **New York: Clarion.**

In this Newbery Honor book, Catherine writes in her diary about her struggles for identity and independence against a mother determined to make a medieval lady of her and against the suitors who do not suit her.

**Cleaver, Vera, and Bill Cleaver. 1969.** *Where the Lillies Bloom.* **New York: HarperCollins.**

In the backwoods of Appalachia, fourteen-year-old Mary Call and her siblings have to combine their talents to survive when their father dies and they are left orphans.

**Ferris, Jean. 1989. *Looking for Home*. New York: Farrar, Straus, Giroux.**

When Daphne finds herself pregnant before her senior year, she leaves school, leaves her dysfunctional family, moves to a new city, and creates a new kind of family.

**Robinet, Harriette. 1995. *If You Please, President Lincoln*. New York: Atheneum (Jean Karl).**

Christmas, 1883. Fourteen-year-old Moses runs away from his master and thinks he is on his way to a new life when he joins a group of other former slaves headed for a small island near Haiti. True to his name, with the support of his blind friend, Goshen, Moses becomes a leader and helps the group survive in the face of incredible odds. He tells their story, one grounded in historical fact, once they are rescued.

# Honor

**Avi. 1990. *The True Confessions of Charlotte Doyle*. New York: Orchard.**

In 1832, Charlotte, en route to America to join her family, finds herself enmeshed in a mutiny plot and has a series of adventures which force her to determine her values.

**Crutcher, Chris. 1983. *Running Loose*. New York: Greenwillow.**

When Louie is a senior, his coach asks him to "play dirty," which Louie refuses to do. He then has to face the consequences of this decision to follow his conscience rather than the dictates of the crowd.

**Peck, Robert Newton. 1973. *A Day No Pigs Would Die*. New York: Alfred Knopf.**

Rob has to grow up quickly when he helps butcher his pet pig, who is barren, and then he has to become man of the family when he learns his father, too, will no longer be with them.

**Taylor, Theodore. 1995. *The Bomb*. New York: Harcourt Brace.**

Sorry and his family, inhabitants of Bikini Atoll, are told by the Americans that they will have to relocate, because their "liberators" want to do more testing of the kind of bomb they have recently dropped on

Hiroshima. Sorry, his uncle, and his teacher distrust the Americans—their tests and their promises—and they plot to defy the U.S. military, with tragic results in this haunting tale, based on a little-known piece of history, about the costs of war and its weapons.

# Environments

**Hobbs, Will. 1992. *The Big Wander*. New York: Atheneum.**

While fourteen-year-old Clay is searching through a canyon in the Southwest for his uncle, he becomes involved with a group of Navajo Indians trying to save some of the last wild mustangs.

**Johnston, Norma. 1994. *The Image Game*. New York: Bridgewater Books.**

Two high school students make themselves over to get parents off their backs, but in the process they discover the dangers of not being themselves and they discover some difficult truths about the relationship between a local company and the town.

**Reaver, Chap. 1994. *Bill*. New York: Delacorte.**

Thirteen-year-old Jessica and her dog, Bill, have to figure out whom they can trust when her father, a maker of moonshine in the Kentucky backwoods, is arrested by the local revenue agent.

# Immigration

**Guy, Rosa. 1973. *The Friends*. New York: Henry Holt.**

Phyllisia, a recent immigrant to Harlem from the West Indies, and Edith, a "ragamuffin," form a realistic and deep friendship that crosses cultural boundaries, in spite of Phyllisia's family's concerns.

**Uchida, Yoshiko. 1991. *Invisible Thread*. New York: Julian Messner.**

This is Uchida's autobiography of her life as a Japanese American growing up in California.

**Yep, Laurence. 1979. *The Sea Glass*. New York: HarperCollins.**

A young Chinese boy has to confront his father, who wants him to be an athlete; Yep says that this story is his most autobiographical.

# Origins

**Irwin, Hadley. 1987. *Kim/Kimi*. New York: Margaret K. McElderry (Macmillan).**

At sixteen, Kim Andrews decides she needs to find out more about her Japanese father's family, but then, as she discovers some unsettling truths about the detention camps where Japanese Americans were held against their will during World War II, she has to wonder whether or not his family will ever be able to accept her mixed ancestry.

**Lasky, Kathryn. 1990. *Traces of Life: The Origins of Human Kind*. New York: William Morrow.**

Lasky presents the research of six paleoanthropologists into the questions of why and how the human evolutionary tract diverged from that of the apes.

**Mazer, Norma Fox. 1995. *Missing Pieces*. New York: Morrow.**

Trying to complete a family history project for school, Jessie asks her mother for information about her missing father; her mother is fiercely reluctant to provide it, so Jessie sets off on a quest to find out about her father—and finds out about herself in the process.

**Myers, Walter Dean. 1994. *The Glory Field*. New York: Scholastic.**

Myers details the life of one member of the Lewis family from each of six generations, all bound together by their ownership of "The Glory Field," describing their various struggles with issues of race, survival, and identity.

**Rinaldi, Ann. 1991. *Wolf by the Ears*. New York: Scholastic.**

At twenty-one, Harriet Hemmings, a slave at Monticello, is freed, and then must decide whether to "pass" in the White world or to stay in the more familiar world in which she has grown up.

**Wyeth, Sharon Dennis. 1994. *The World of Daughter McGuire*. New York: Delacorte.**

Daughter McGuire is called a "zebra" by the members of the Avengers because of her biracial heritage, but she also learns that she has Jewish, Russian, Italian, Irish, and African blood in her background. She learns, too, that she inherited some of courage of the woman for whom she was named.

# War

These titles are annotated in Chapter 4, "Conflict and Confrontation."

Choi, Sook Nyul. 1993. *Echoes of the White Giraffe*. Boston: Houghton Mifflin.

Hunt, Irene. 1964. *Across Five Aprils*. River Grove, IL: Follett.

Miklowitz, Gloria D. 1985. *The War Between the Classes*. New York: Delacorte.

Westall, Robert. 1992. *Gulf*. London: Methuen Children's Books.

## Influences

Bornstein, Sandy. 1989. *What Makes You What You Are? A First Look at Genetics*. New York: Julian Messner.

Bornstein's easy-to-follow text helps readers understand the role genetics plays in determining such attributes as hair color or height and weight.

Davis, Jenny. 1987. *Good-bye and Keep Cold*. New York: Orchard.

After Edda's father dies in a strip-mining accident, Edda tries to take care of everyone, but she ultimately has to learn that she can really only take responsibility for her own life.

Hinton, S. E. 1967. *The Outsiders*. New York: Viking.

Ponyboy Curtis explains his family situation, his brothers' personalities, Johnny's death, and the conflict between the "Socs" and the "Greasers," offering his interpretations of why things are the way they are.

Myers, Walter Dean. 1988. *Scorpions*. New York: HarperCollins.

There are a multitude of influences operating on Jamal Hicks that eventually lead him into trouble with the Scorpions, a gang formerly led by his brother, and with the law.

## Confrontation

These titles are annotated in Chapter 4, "Conflict and Confrontation."

Naidoo, Beverly. 1990. *Chain of Fire*. Philadelphia: Lippincott.

Namioka, Lensey. 1994. *April and the Dragon Lady*. New York: Browndeer Press (Harcourt Brace).

Strasser, Todd. 1985. *A Very Touchy Subject*. New York: Delacorte.

# Freedom

**Hamilton, Virginia. 1988.** *Anthony Burns: The Defeat and Triumph of a Fugitive Slave.* **New York: Alfred Knopf.**

Hamilton tells the true story of twenty-year-old slave Anthony Burns, who escaped to Boston in 1854, but who was then captured by his owner, causing thousands of abolitionists to rise to his defense.

**Lowry, Lois. 1989.** *Number the Stars.* **Boston: Houghton Mifflin.**

Ten-year-old Annemarie fears for the life of Ellen, her best friend, who happens to be Jewish, when the German soldiers take control of Denmark in 1943. She takes some drastic actions to help ensure her friend's survival.

**Peck, Robert Newton. 1989.** *Arly.* **New York: Walker.**

During the 1920s, Arly, his father, and their friends, poor field workers, are virtually prisoners of the landowner of Jailtown until a new school teacher comes to town and provides hope for a better future.

# Color

**Mori, Kyoko. 1993.** *Shizuko's Daughter.* **New York: Henry Holt.**

When her artist mother dies, twelve-year-old Yuki feels as if the color has been drained from her world; eventually, she experiences the transforming power of art, and finds a way to add color to her life once more.

**Oneal, Zibby. 1985.** *In Summer Light.* **New York: Viking/Kestral.**

As sixteen-year-old Kate struggles to find her own way as an artist, competing with feelings of inadequacy because of her father's artistic reputation, she describes the ways in which she uses color and light to express herself.

**Porte, Barbara. 1987.** *I Only Made Up the Roses.* **New York: Greenwillow.**

Cindra's father is Black and her mother is White, and in her journal, Cindra narrates what this mix of colors means to her and her unusual family.

# Space

**Cisneros, Sandra. 1989.** *The House on Mango Street.* **New York: Vintage.**

The Hispanic American narrator of these vignettes describes life in the cramped house on Mango Street and tells of her longing for a different kind of environment.

**Holland, Isabelle. 1978.** *Dinah and the Green Fat Kingdom.* **Philadelphia: Lippincott.**

Twelve-year-old Dinah, tired of being nagged about her weight, creates a space for herself, a refuge she ultimately can leave when she finds some new friends, and begins to take charge of her life.

**Smith, Robert Kimmel. 1984.** *The War with Grandpa.* **New York: Delacorte.**

Pete's parents tell him he must give up his much-treasured room to his grandfather, and Pete vows war in order to reclaim it.

# Frontiers

**Hudson, Jan. 1989.** *Sweetgrass.* **New York: Philomel.**

Sweetgrass, a fifteen-year-old Blackfoot girl, is unhappy with the role of women, with her parents, with her brother, but she still helps her tribe survive smallpox and a very difficult winter.

**Mohr, Nicholassa. 1973.** *Nilda.* **New York: HarperCollins.**

The racial hatred Nilda experiences as a Puerto Rican girl growing up in 1940s New York City creates a different sense of boundary and frontier than that associated with the wide open plains of the American West.

**Taylor, Mildred. 1990.** *The Road to Memphis.* **New York: Dial.**

Now a high school senior, Cassie, whom readers first met in *Roll of Thunder, Hear My Cry*, confronts the boundaries of racism yet again when violence erupts in her Mississippi town, and she has to decide whether to help the victim flee the state.

**Taylor, Theodore. 1986.** *Walking up a Rainbow: Being the Version of the Long and Hazardous Journey of Susan D. Carlisle, Mrs. Myrtle Dessery, Drover Bert Pettit, and Cowboy Clay Carmer and Others.* **New York: Delacorte.**

Taylor's lengthy title accurately portrays what happens in this western.

# Boundaries

**Filipovic, Zlata. 1994.** *Zlata's Diary.* **Trans. Christina Pribichevih-Zoric. New York: Viking.**

Just before her eleventh birthday Zlata begins this diary, which she keeps for two years, detailing the dramatic changes in her life when war erupts over boundary lines in her hometown of Sarajevo.

**Dickinson, Peter. 1994.** *Shadow of Hero.* **New York: Delacorte.**

After the fall of communism and in the midst of the chaos then prevalent in Eastern Europe, a determined few, including Restaur Vax and his granddaughter, struggle to keep the invented country Varina from the tragic fate of Bosnia and Croatia.

**Konigsburg, E. L. 1982.** *Journey to an 800 Number.* **New York: Atheneum.**

When Maximillian's mother leaves for a long honeymoon, he goes to stay with his father, Woody, and begins to explore the artificial boundaries imposed by social class distinctions.

**Staples, Suzanne Fisher. 1989.** *Shabanu: Daughter of the Wind.* **New York: Alfred Knopf.**

'Shabanu, twelve, and her family are nomads of the Cholistan Desert, but their lives are changing because of the property lines others are imposing.

# Beliefs

**Nelson, Theresa. 1994.** *Earthshine.* **New York: Orchard.**

Slim struggles with her beliefs about life and death as she watches her charismatic father dying of AIDS.

**Peck, Richard. 1995.** *The Last Safe Place on Earth.* **New York: Delacorte.**

Walden Woods is a community both racist and sexist in subtle ways that believes itself to be a safe haven, but censorship efforts on the part of the Christian right challenge the status quo, and sophomore Todd Tobin learns "there is no safe place."

**Ruby, Lois. 1994.** *Skin Deep.* **New York: Scholastic.**

A lonely young man, his self-esteem very low, is swept into the world of the Skinheads, but he finally pulls himself away and attempts to figure out his own perspective on racial issues.

**Rylant, Cynthia. 1989.** *A Fine White Dust.* **New York: Bradbury.**

Pete is first saved, then befriended, and ultimately betrayed by the Preacher Man who comes to his town, but he finally decides that he still believes God to be a significant factor in his life.

# Order

**Block, Francesca Lia. 1989.** *Weetzie Bat.* **New York: HarperCollins.**

This spoof of Hollywood reality violates readers' expectations of an orderly story line and realistic characters, and yet conveys a strong message about the nature of love and family.

**Freedman, Russell. 1988.** *Buffalo Hunt.* **New York: Holiday House.**

Russell Freedman describes the buffalo's role in the spiritual life and hunts of Native Americans living on the Great Plains, noting the sense of order these hunters perceived in the universe.

**Fox, Paula. 1985.** *Moonlight Man.* **New York: Bradbury.**

Catherine's father, who drinks too much, is nevertheless a charming and endearing "moonlight man," but Catherine has to switch roles, becoming the grown-up in the family, and she wonders whether the alcohol will destroy the tenuousness of their father/daughter relationship.

**Scoppetone, Sandra. 1974.** *Trying Hard to Hear You.* **New York: Harper and Row.**

Camilla's world is turned upside down when she finds out that the boy with whom she is infatuated is involved with another young man.

# Sources

**Meyer, Caroline. 1994.** *Rio Grande Stories.* **New York: Harcourt Brace.**

The seventh grade at Rio Grande Middle School decides to raise money for their school by writing and selling a book about their varied heritages as influenced by the region of New Mexico in which they live.

**Lipsyte, Robert. 1991.** *The Brave.* **New York: HarperCollins.**

Alfred Brooks, of *The Contender,* is now a police officer in New York, where he meets and befriends Sonny Bear, a Moscondaga Indian searching to allow the Hawk spirit of his people into his heart.

**Hamilton, Virginia. 1967.** *Zeely.* **New York: Macmillan.**

Geeder, an imaginative eleven-year-old, becomes enchanted by the beauty and strength of a Watutsi queen, whom she convinces herself must be related to a local woman, Zeely; as the novel unfolds, Geeder gains a sense of pride from her growing knowledge of the Watutsi heritage.

# Rights

**Danziger, Paula. 1974.** *The Cat Ate My Gymsuit.* **New York: Delacorte.**

Marcy and her friends learn a good deal about civil rights when they go up against the school board in an effort to reverse the decision to fire their favorite teacher.

**Green, Bette. 1991.** *The Drowning of Stephan Jones.* **New York: Bantam.**

Carla's infatuation with Andy has caused her to become a silent partner in his hate campaign against a gay couple, but when Andy's behavior goes too far, Carla has to decide, before the trial, what she believes and what justice means.

**Hentoff, Nat. 1987.** *The Day They Came to Arrest the Book.* **New York: Delacorte.**

Barney Roth, editor of the high school paper, decides to take a stand when a group of students and parents demands that *The Adventures of Huckleberry Finn* be removed from the school library.

**Krisher, Trudy. 1994.** *Spite Fences.* **New York: Delacorte.**

Thirteen-year-old Maggie, from Kinship, Georgia, has always just accepted the fences that separate rich and poor, Black and White, but when Zeke gives her a camera and teaches her about "never being afraid of the truth," Maggie has to question those fences and make some difficult decisions.

# Cycles

**Craven, Margaret. 1973. *I Heard the Owl Call My Name*. New York: Doubleday.**

A young, terminally ill priest is sent by his superior to live in a remote Indian village so that he can learn from them about the nature of life and death.

**Johnson, Angela. 1993. *Toning the Sweep*. New York: Orchard (Richard Jackson).**

Three generations of African American women learn together some of the truths about the natural cycle of life and death.

**Lynch, Chris. 1994. *Gypsy Davey*. New York: HarperCollins.**

Can Davey break the cycle of abuse in his family, or is he destined to live the same kind of life that his mother and sister have had?

**Paterson, Katherine. 1980. *Jacob Have I Loved*. New York: Crowell.**

The cycles of life and death, of the tide, of life on the water underpin this story of Louise's efforts to find peace within herself and to conquer the jealousy she has always felt for her twin sister.

# Behavior

**Cormier, Robert. 1974. *The Bumblebee Flies Anyway*. New York: Pantheon.**

Young adults with terminal illness are the objects of experiments in this novel which explores the results of threats to the social order.

**Sleator, William. 1974. *House of Stairs*. New York: Dutton.**

In an elaborate Skinnerian experiment, a group of young people struggle against the ways in which they are being manipulated by external forces.

**———. 1984. *Interstellar Pig*. New York: Dutton.**

Evil aliens move into the beach house next door to the one Barney's parents have rented, and they begin to exert a tremendous influence on his life.

**Voigt, Cynthia. 1985.** *The Runner.* **New York: Atheneum.**

Why does Bullet Tillerman run, and how will he react now that there is a new runner, an African American, on the team?

# Tradition

**Manes, Stephen. 1988.** *The Obnoxious Jerks.* **New York: Bantam.**

A bunch of high school guys are out to upset the status quo in their high school, but how will they react when a girl wants to join their exclusive group, violating their own traditions?

**Smith, Ruckshanna. 1982.** *Sumitra's Story.* **New York: Coward-McCann.**

Sumitra must choose between the traditions of India and her family and the opportunities afforded to her as a bright young woman in London.

**Schami, Rafik. 1990.** *A Handful of Stars.* **Trans. Rika Lesser. New York: Dutton.**

The narrator of this story lives in Syria, where censorship problems are great and tradition may keep him from his dream of becoming a journalist.

# Home

These titles are annotated in Chapter 2, "There's No Place Like Home."

**Cleary, Beverly. 1983.** *Dear Mr. Henshaw.* **New York: William Morrow Junior Books.**

**Fox, Paula. 1991.** *Monkey Island.* **New York: Orchard (Richard Jackson).**

**MacLachlan, Patricia. 1991.** *Journey.* **New York: Doubleday.**

**Myers, Walter Dean. 1992.** *Somewhere in the Darkness.* **New York: Scholastic.**

**Paterson, Katherine. 1978.** *The Great Gilly Hopkins.* **New York: Crowell.**

**Rylant, Cynthia. 1992.** *Missing May.* **New York: Orchard.**

**Spinelli, Jerry. 1990.** *Maniac McGee.* **Boston: Little, Brown.**

# A Selected List of Useful Resources

In addition to the reviews of young adult literature regularly published in professional journals such as *The ALAN Review, Booklist, The Hornbook, The English Journal, The Reading Teacher, School Library Journal, The New Advocate, Teaching Tolerance, The Wilson Library Bulletin,* and *VOYA* (Voices of Youth Advocates), the following titles provide a wealth of information about books written for young adults.

Ahmed, Ali Jimale, and Irving L. Markovitz. 1993. "African Literature and Social Science in the Teaching of World Studies." Social Studies 84(2): 78–81.

Anderson, Vicki. 1994. Immigrants in the United States in Fiction: A Guide to 705 Books for Librarians and Teachers, K–9. ERIC Document ED371931.

Brown, Jean E., and Elaine C. Stephens. 1995. *Teaching Young Adult Literature: Sharing the Connections.* Belmont, CA: Wadsworth Publishing.

Burnaford, Gail. 1993. "The Challenge of Integrated Curricula." *Music Educators Journal* 79(9): 44–47.

Bushman, John H., and Kay Parks Bushman. 1993. *Using Young Adult Literature in the English Classroom.* New York: Merrill.

Carter, Betty, ed. 1994. *Best Books for Young Adults: The Selections, the History, the Romance.* Chicago: American Library Association.

Caywood, Carolyn. 1993. "Computers in Fiction." *Voice of Youth Advocates* 16(5): 275–78.

Galda, Lee, and Pat MacGregor. 1992. "Nature's Wonders: Books for a Science Curriculum." *Reading Teacher* 46(3): 236–45.

Kaywell, Joan F., ed. 1993. 1995. *Adolescent Literature as a Complement to the Classics.* Vol. I and II. Norwood, MA: Christopher-Gordon.

Kaywell, Joan F. 1993. *Adolescents at Risk: A Guide to Fiction and Nonfiction for Young Adults, Parents, and Professionals.* Westport, CT: Greenwood Press.

Miller-Lachman, Lyn, ed. 1992. *Our Family, Our Friends, Our World: An Annotated Guide to Significant Multicultural Books for Children and Teenagers.* New Providence, NJ: R. R. Bowker.

Monseau, Virginia R. 1996. *Responding to Young Adult Literature.* Portsmouth, NH: Boynton/Cook.

Monseau, Virginia R., and Gary M. Salvner, eds. 1992. *Reading Their World: The Young Adult Novel in the Classroom.* Portsmouth, NH: Boynton/Cook.

Moore, John Noell. 1997. *Interpreting Young Adult Literature: Literacy Theory in the Classroom.* Portsmouth, NH: Boynton/Cook.

Moss, Joy F. 1994. *Using Literature in the Middle Grades: A Thematic Approach.* Norwood, MA: Christopher-Gordon.

National Council of Teachers of English. *The NCTE Bibliography Series* (includes *Adventuring with Books: A Booklist for Pre–K–Grade 6; Books for You: A Booklist for Senior High School Students; High Interest, Easy Reading: A Booklist for Junior and Senior High School Students; Your Reading: A Booklist for Junior High and Middle School Students*). Urbana, IL: National Council of Teachers of English. (New editions available approximately every three years.)

Nilsen, Alleen Pace, and Kenneth L. Donelson. 1993. *Literature for Today's Young Adults.* 4th ed. New York: HarperCollins College Publishers.

Reed, Arthea J. S. 1994. *Comics to Classics: A Guide to Books for Teens and Preteens.* New York: Penguin.

Rochman, Hazel. 1993. *Against Borders: Promoting Books for a Multicultural World.* Chicago: American Library Association.

Spencer, Pam, ed. 1994. *What Do Young Adults Read Next? A Reader's Guide to Fiction for Young Adults.* Washington, DC: Gale Research, Inc.

Stringer, Sharon. 1997. *The Young Adult Novel and Adolescent Psychology.* Portsmouth, NH: Boynton/Cook.

Sullivan, Arlene. 1993. *Death in Literature for Children and Young Adults: Focused Access to Selected Topics.* ERIC Document ED356485.

Tchudi, Stephen, ed. 1993. *The Astonishing Curriculum: Integrating Science and Humanities Through Language.* Urbana, IL: National Council of Teachers of English.